Splitting Hairs

THE BALD TRUTH ABOUT
BAD HAIR DAYS

Written and illustrated by Mimi Pond

A FIRESIDE BOOK PUBLISHED BY SIMON & SCHUSTER

FIRESIDE

Rockefeller Center 1230 Avenue of the Americas, New York, NY 10020

Copyright © 1998 by Mimi Pond

FIRESIDE and colophon are registered trademarks of Simon & Schuster Inc.

Designed by Leah Lococo

Manufactured in the United States of America

1 3 5 7 9 10 8 6 4 2

Library of Congress Cataloging-in-Publication Data

Pond, Mimi. Splitting hairs: the bald truth about bad hair days/
written and illustrated by Mimi Pond.

p. cm.

A Fireside book.

1. Hairstyles—Humor. 2. Hair—Humor. 3. Hairdressing—Humor.

I. Title.

GT2290.P66   1998

391.5'02'07—dc21   98-39863   CIP

ISBN 0-684-82643-7

This book is dedicated to everyone
who was willing to talk to me about their pathetic/
neurotic/bizarre/sad/funny hair experiences
—even if they did mostly want to be anonymous
—they all have my heartfelt thanks.

CONTENTS

INTRODUCTION

It's right there on top of your head, ready, willing, and able to make a fool of you unless you master it in some way. It's hair, and it's funny. Hair is the biggest symbol of anxiety that we possess. Those who know what to do with it are admired, envied, and usually resented by those who don't. Everyone, hairy or bald, vain or oblivious, has had, at the very least, a passing fear about their hair. Some change their dos at the drop of a hat. Others don't and stick stubbornly with one hairstyle their whole lives through. There is always a lingering worry, in the back of everyone's head, so to speak, that it could be better or, at least, different. After all, when you take off your clothes, your hair is the only thing left on you, a "kick me" sign attached to your flesh.

CHAPTER ONE

Hair Neurosis

Don't try to deny it. HAIR RULE NUMBER ONE: *Your hair is a source of anxiety.* It sits right on top of your head where everyone can see it and think to themselves, "Does she comb her hair with a pasta fork?" Or, "Poor dear, I suppose she's just given up." You can spend years and bucketfuls of money trying to find the right look. Then, even when you think you've achieved it, striding confidently from the salon, there's the quietly paranoid sensation that what you see is not what other people see. You can go insane. Oh, there are the few among us who have perfect hair, but these are celebrities who have professionals constantly hovering over them. If it's any consolation though, celebrities are even more anxious about their hair than you are, because often their hair is the sum total of who they are.

Is it any wonder we're all so paranoid about our hair?

BANGS! YOU'RE DEAD

Bangs are just the beginning of hair anxiety. Who hasn't suffered the fate of too-short bangs, bangs that make you look shocked, surprised, and well . . . like someone who's been institutionalized but somehow managed to get ahold of some surgical scissors?

MORON

CRETIN

JULIUS CAESAR CRETIN

THE HDA

Of course, our hair anxiety stems from the fact that, in this world, making fun of other people's hair is a recognized spectator sport. Some have a secret code to alert their friends to a hairdo in their immediate vicinity—an HDA (Hairdo Alert). However, HAIR RULE NUMBER TWO: *If you are a true hair spectator, all bad hair will find you.* The HDA's in the world will eventually find themselves in an airport while you are stuck there for eight hours without anything to read. It's just that, at an airport with time on your hands, every unisex Billy Ray Cyrus variation imaginable, those rattails on small boys, the old white ladies with Afros, the gals who *still* have those petrified Farrah wings framing their faces, the men who've managed to sculpt for themselves completely transparent combover pompadours have all gathered here, apparently just to drive you crazy.

At the airport, the mall, on the bus, in the post office line— this is where you get the impulse to become a hairdresser and just fix everyone's major hair faux pas. But then, to do that, you have to attend a seedy vocational school, also known as beauty college, also known as a beauty institute, with a bunch of scary, chain-smoking, rattailed comb-wielding, eyeliner-masked re- form-school graduates, all named Anita or Tina; practice finger waves on severed mannequin heads; learn about diseases of the

Animal, Vegetable, or Mineral:
HAIR THAT LOOKS LIKE SOMETHING ELSE

OLD TOAST

CAKE FROSTING

A DOLL LEFT OUT IN THE YARD

COTTON CANDY

COUCH STUFFING

AN AFGHAN HOUND

A STRAY CAT

BOZO'S WIG

FAKE FUR

A MOP

OLD ROPE

SAUSAGE

scalp; graduate; somehow obtain a license; get a salon job, just so you can stand on your feet all day and put up with a bunch of neurotic whining, complaining crybabies all day long who want to yak about themselves and wonder why you can't make them look like their favorite TV star. Yes, you really have to be a crusader to want to fix all the bad hair in the world.

HAIR:

The Resonating Touchstone of Memory

Poor, poor Proust. If only he had known that the stupid little cookie he wrote about was nothing compared to hair. What about the sense memories contained within the aroma of a Toni home perm? The instant recall in a noseful of Alberto VO5? The angst of adolescence that comes rushing back in a veil of Aqua Net?

* Mom designated one sister the long-haired one and one as the short-haired one, and annoyingly, thirty years later, it's still stuck.

* Watching Cousin Jetta roll her hair on orange juice cans and worship-

ing her as a goddess, she vowed
to have the biggest hair on the planet.

* Driving across Texas on long car trips, he
  and his sister would sit in the back seat
  and take turns sticking things in the back
  of Mama's giant hairdo to pass the time.

* Sitting in a high chair in the kitchen with a pillowcase fastened
  around his neck with an old diaper pin, Daddy tried to tell his
  son the facts of life while razoring the back of his neck. "Son,"
  he recalls hearing Dad say, "you know, you can't put your penis
  in a woman's flagellum if it's all floppy."

MY FIRST BAD-HAIR DAY

Everyone has had a bad-hair day, but the worst ones happen to
children. They can't communicate what it is they want, or if they
can, the idea is generally vetoed by grown-ups. Is it any wonder
that these memories stay with us our whole lives?

Lousy Timing

Marjorie recalls getting lice at age ten and undergoing the usual
nasty medicated shampoo and fine-toothed comb procedure.

Weeks later, the treatment successful, she went for a sleepover at a friend's house. When Marjorie colorfully related the story of nobly and bravely enduring this harsh treatment to her friend and her friend's mother (pointing out the fact that she didn't even cry), she thought she was casting herself as the heroic, stalwart survivor of a horrible fate. She was then surprised to find herself quickly packed up and driven home in her pajamas.

The Curtain-O-Hair

Al Hoff recalls a San Francisco childhood of pathetic hair and miserable yearning. She would stand in the beaded curtain doorway  of her closet, pretend she was Cher, and practice the patented one-finger, two-finger Cher hair flick. She also says she would gaze at the long-hair wigs in the cheap-hooker wig store at Powell and Market. Says Al, "I longed to have the strength to wear one. Imagine that Jan Brady had more guts than me!"

Not Sally Bowles

Ann relates that when she was in the fifth grade, after the movie *Cabaret* came out, her mother, apparently inspired by the prewar decadence of Berlin, told the beautician to give her daughter a "Liza" cut. Ann did not resemble Miss Minnelli. The asymmetrical spit curls plastered to her cheeks only served to emphasize her glasses and braces. There was much weeping.

Minute Maid

Marcy R. reports that when she was fifteen and living in Miami, she performed a particular classic teenage ritual in order to make her unruly, frizzy hair up-to-the-moment, long, perfectly straight, parted-down-the-middle Marsha Brady hair. The ritual involved rolling the hair on top of her head on two large-size Minute Maid orange juice cans and then taking the hair from the sides of her head and wrapping it completely around her head, plastering that with Dippity-Do and pinning it down with long clips (but not too many, because she didn't want dents). One afternoon, she had performed this elaborate toilette and was in the kitchen getting some juice when her older brother and his friends, upon whom she had crushes, walked in. They teased her mercilessly, flicking at the cans atop her head, completely humiliated her, and drove her to tears. Ironically, a few years later, after she allowed her hair to go wild and natural, her brother's same friends began to ask her out. Did she date them? No.

OUR WORST HAIR EXPERIENCES:
Walking Nightmares

Town Without Pity

Helene reports that, soon after she moved to Los Angeles from New Jersey, she was referred to a hairdresser in a posh West Hollywood salon. The hairdresser kept her waiting for an hour, then dragged her outside to the barren, asphalt parking lot, where, under a pitiless California sun, he disgustedly examined her locks. He told her that he couldn't touch her hair unless she allowed him to color it first. She told him she didn't want to color her hair. He accused her of wasting both their time and turned on his heel. Helene felt humiliated and angry. She didn't know what his problem was, but later she was pleased to learn that he had to go to the Betty Ford clinic for it.

Just Two Words

I never expected my bad-hair day to fall on an afternoon when I, in desperate need of color and a trim, was instead preoccupied with chasing a two-year-old around an art museum. When I picked her up, her screams of defiance filled the gallery, and as I looked around for my husband to tell him I was taking her outside, I drew a withering glance from an older, perfectly groomed, perfectly dressed, obviously childless woman. "She's two," I threw over my shoulder defensively as I walked by. "Well," the woman said, "she ought to be outside." "I'm just looking for my husband—" I began, wondering why I even needed to give her any explanation. He came by and wordlessly took my daughter out, leaving our four-year-old son with me. "Children don't belong in museums," she pronounced airily, gesturing toward my son, who was absorbed in a painting, "I feel sorry for your son. He obviously doesn't want to be here." I was sputtering with anger. "You have no idea—" I began. "Why didn't you just get a baby-sitter?" she asked. "You don't know what you're talking about," I said through clenched teeth. She gave me a pitying look, up and down, and then she said, condescendingly, "Oh . . . why don't you just go get your hair done?" It was then that I found myself screaming, in the middle of a crowded art museum, "FUCK YOU!"

PEOPLE WHO FLIP:

Annoying Hair Tics

The Male Long-Hair Flip

A more or less constant tossing of the head, without the hands, that says nothing if not, "I'm too cool to touch my hair, so I'll just keep jerking my head around to keep it out of my eyes."

The Phantom Flip

Seen in teenage boys who have gone from long hair to a crewcut, but by now the tic is completely involuntary.

The Bar Flip

The apparently casual act of running the fingers through the hair in the front of the head and tossing it back. It's usually performed by women sitting alone in cocktail lounges who are trying to telegraph this information: "I must appear to be completely bored and utterly unattainable, but my hair is begging you to buy my head a drink."

Neurotic Hair Twisting

See Diane Keaton in *Annie Hall*. This isn't so much a tic as an annoying attention-getting device that says, "Aren't I adorably child-like and cute?"

The Look-at-My-Beautiful-Hair Tic

People of both sexes who constantly run their fingers across their heads apparently can't get over their own beautiful hair.

The Patented Cher Flick

See reruns of *The Sonny and Cher Show* on cable for a demonstration of this unique, casually executed, one-finger, two-finger flick that keeps Cher's ass-length hair from getting tangled in her arms and fingers and thus ruining the dramatic moment while she throatily sings such classics as "Gypsies, Tramps and Thieves" and "Half-Breed."

OW, YOU'RE ON MY HAIR

Hair is an aphrodisiac that becomes a logistical nightmare in bed. How can you achieve multiple orgasm when a guy's got his elbows on your locks, and it feels like your scalp is being ripped off your skull?

Marjorie said her neck is extremely ticklish, and should a stray hair happen to graze that area during what is supposed to be a passionate kiss, she will burst out laughing, completely ruining the moment. But who doesn't do that anyway?

Practical Alison remembers that, in high school, to avoid getting a rat's nest on the back of her head, she would always put her hair in pigtails before sex. I asked, "So did word get around school that if you were wearing pigtails, it was—how shall I say—open season?" She giggled, turned beet red, shook her head, and added, "It's just that I used to worry so much about how my hair looked during sex that I'd get completely distracted."

Marlene, a real firecracker of a Texas Big Hair Gal, tells us about the Curtain of Jesus. "I thought of this my first year of college, when I first started giving bl—, I mean performing, uh, oral sex," she says. "First, you take the scrunchy out of your nice long hair and your hair just falls around and covers everything, so while you're doin' it, it's the Curtain of Jesus, you're cloaked in mystery, you don't have to think about what it actually is, I mean, you could pretend you're sucking on a popsicle or somethin.' " She takes a breath, then continues. "I mean, I usta worry about my friends with short hair. I'd think, 'They have to be totally conscious about what they're doin', ee-ew, how can they stand it?' " Marlene adds, "That's why I've never had short hair. Never, never."

When I asked Ophelia if she had any sex-related hair stories, she said, "Uh . . . does it have to be hair on the head?" "Why?" I asked. "Because this guy I dated once gave me a gift. A brown pa-per bag. When I opened it up, it was full of hair. Turned out he had shaved his whole body, from the neck down, and gave me the hair as a gift." I stared at her, open-mouthed. "We broke up pretty soon after that," she said, defensively. "Pretty soon?" I said.

THE LONG AND THE SHORT OF IT

For some it's an endless debate, for others, no question. Should I wear it long or short? If it's long, it may just lay there like a Portuguese man-of-war on your head, limp and slack, unless you take the labor-intensive, arm-wearying, time-consuming initiative. If it's short, is it just a copout? Will you look like some prepubescent gymnast-turned-minivan-driving, pastel jogging-suit-clad housewife? Not if you dye it green. But then there's the fear of being the artsy type with the crew cut and the big wacky earrings. But as you get older, you fear, even more, looking like Jerry Garcia's first wife, Mountain Girl.

Should 95 percent of long-haired women mention to their significant male others that they're thinking of cutting it short, you'd think from their response that these women were planning a sex change. Polled, most men, even down to that weird guy who comes around your office selling muffins out of a Styrofoam

The Pros and Cons of Short Hair

PRO	CON

JUST WASH IT AND GO	STEP MISSING IN VANITY RITUAL

CAN'T GET INTO TOO MUCH TROUBLE UP THERE	ALL MEN FEEL PERSONALLY BETRAYED BY YOU

IN GOOD MOOD FEEL LIKE LESLIE CARON	IN BAD MOOD FEEL LIKE GERTRUDE STEIN

cooler, will always beg, "Don't cut your hair!" This plays on a woman's fears that with the flick of the scissors, she'll look like a hulking, crew-cutted prison matron—Ernest Borgnine with a mammary problem. "Is that all he sees of me? What am I, a walking wig stand?" If she asks other women, a good 80 percent will say, "Cut it. And then," this phrase is somehow fixed in their minds, "you can just wash it and go!"

HAIR COLOR AND IDENTITY

The stereotypes are still in place. Redheads have bad tempers, blondes are dumb, brunettes are . . . uh . . . they have brown hair. Since women, and today even men, can and do change their hair color at the drop of a hat, these assumptions are even sillier than ever. The idea that you are your hair color, even if it's lurking under a dye job, is the deep, almost unconscious suspicion of many.

It's a Blond Thing: You Wouldn't Understand

There is a certain, almost mystical fascination about blondes, as though they were a separate species, but what are we really talking about, anyway? Less pigment. Fewer follicles. More actual hairs on the head. Big deal. And those are the ones who come by it honestly. This obsession seems silly, given that anybody can *become* a blonde. (Although there ought to be a bottle law, because, clearly, not everyone was meant to be blond. That would include people whose skin is yellow enough as it is, or people whose personalities are already out of control.) Blondness is more an attitude than anything else. Blondes seem to get away with murder. There are those blondes who steal your boyfriends. Those blondes who turn men instantly into babbling idiots. Those blondes who laugh at any stupid joke a guy tells just to confirm her blondness. However, there are blondes, and then there are *blondes*. Sharon Stone is the kind of blonde we like. Neither an ice maiden nor a bitch goddess, Sharon's a democratic party girl who whips the soiree into a fever pitch and then, when she senses things have peaked, spontaneously hatches

a plan for a road trip and takes you along in her vintage Mustang because she likes your attitude. On the trip, since she attracts guys like a platinum magnet, there's bound to be spillover. When you get in a bind, Sharon's the one who—surprise!—has a gun in her purse. Unlike Thelma and Louise, you make it to the border, because

Sharon, unlike Louise, wouldn't mind driving through Texas. Of course, safe in Acapulco, you laugh about the whole thing over ice cold cervezas; you haven't paid for your own drinks once on this trip, because you're with Sharon!

Why men lose their minds over *just the idea* of a blonde may have something to do with Sharon Stone. It's the idea that if you are with the *blond one,* life will simply open up before you—no busy signals, no red lights, no traffic jams. An open road to fabulousness. We asked our friend, writer Lynn Peril, who has lived both as a brunette and, briefly, as one of *them.* About her life as a blonde, she wrote, "Male friends, co-workers, and complete strangers began to look at me in much the same way that Homer Simpson regards a donut, with a fatalistic sense of longing in their eyes, and a string of drool hanging down their chins. In other words, it wasn't about me at all. It was about my hair and their fantasies about my hair. That I was attached to my hair was a mere formality."

The power that blondes have over men can be used for good or evil. The choice is yours. Choose your shade carefully. You can go with the expensive, every four weeks, four hours in the salon, multiple-shading technique, but our favorite yellow-haired gals are the do-it-yourself bottle blondes—the ones who have said "No!"

to nature and chosen a destiny with dark roots. Dark roots are the hirsute equivalent of the carelessly exposed bra strap, a way of telling the world, "Yes, I use hair-care products in a cheap and casual manner in order to attract the opposite sex, and I'm probably too much woman for you!" Dark roots tell us they're having too much fun to waste time on a touch-up.

Don't Start with Me: The Redhead Stigma

If you were called "red," "carrottop," "freckles," or "firecracker" from the time you were very small, perhaps you too would develop a sense for just how limited people's imaginations can be. How this could be mistaken for having a bad temper, we'll never know. On the other hand, the constant teases and taunts of friends, enemies, and complete strangers is a character-building experience that often produces a sardonic sense of humor that, in adulthood, can be used as revenge on the world. A world that links those annoying, condescending words "sassy" and "spunky" with "redhead." Then there's that term "torrid redhead." As though having a certain color of hair means that one is in a constant state of estrus. "Torrid"—why, the very word suggests that a girl has to bite her own hand to keep from ripping her clothes off in public. How anyone's deeply complicated and often misunderstood per-sonality could be summed up as "hotheaded" is completely beyond us. But if at any time this is a debate that you would care to have with us, we will gladly tear you a new one.

Brunettes: Nature's Unappreciated Dark Goddesses

Brunettes are the luckiest of all. No one makes assumptions about their personalities or their sexuality based on the color of their hair. If blondes are the one-sentence high concept of hair color, brunettes are complex creatures that can't be described in less than a 750-page epic novel that sweeps continents and spans decades. Think Louise Brooks in *Pandora's Box*, Audrey Hepburn in *Breakfast at Tiffany's*, Barbara Stanwyck in *The Lady Eve*, Liz Taylor in *A Place in the Sun*. Think anything you want. A brunette will always surprise you.

Raven Tresses

A certain ethnic background helps to carry off the fabulousness that is absolutely black hair. Of course, if you're going for the junkie-style, vampirelike decadence of dead-white skin against dead-black hair, that's a different look. But blue-black hair can work in your favor if you're going for the exotic, the mysterious, the sheer inscrutability of blackness.

No Little Old Ladies:
Why Everyone Is Prematurely Gray

People used to fret about gray hairs, but these days, it's just one more choice. If you are among the tiny percentage of people in the world whose skin tones complement gray or white hair, if looking ten years older doesn't bother you, if, in your eighties, you've finally settled on a "mature" look, I say, "Fine! Just go ahead and give up!" For the rest of us, it's open season on "snow on the roof." More power, I say, to elderly women who defy age and all the rules and still dye their hair deepest, deepest jet. Their death-grip on youth is only a bottle away.

HAIR MYSTERY NUMBER ONE: *Why doesn't prematurely gray country-rocker Emmylou Harris just put herself in the hands of a good colorist?*

THE HOME SPA TREATMENT:
Commitment to the Beauty Maintenance Lifestyle

Hair Rituals

No one ever said it was going to be easy. Some people manage to get their daily hair regime down to a three-minute drill. Others

Henna: The Wild Card

You might think of henna as something that eccentric great-aunt of yours has used religiously for the last fifty years; she's the whiskey-voiced one who wears kimonos and chain-smokes using a cigarette holder and still receives gentlemen callers even though she's in her late eighties. Either that, or it's something you put on your hair while you're simultaneously having your tarot read and your I Ching thrown while sitting cross-legged on a pillow made from an Indian bedspread from Pier One. In other words, it's the only sanctioned vanity in an evil world of poisonous chemicals made by the evil corporate consumer establishment for vain dupes easily manipulated by the media. Right on, Sister! Or you might simply perceive henna as the E-Z Bake Oven of hair color, kind of a funny little pretend hair product. But think again. Because, unless you've used henna before successfully, you can never be sure how it's going to turn out, especially if you're putting it on top of another color. Our henna gal-in-the-field, Kathleen, reports having her hair turned several charming shades of seaweed green. Advice from the product's henna hotline only compounded the problem. Professionals, trying numerous times to undo the results with different shades of henna and various other techniques, finally turned Kathleen's hair a vivid magenta. Kathleen finally turned to Miss Clairol for advice. Yes, Henna is truly the Dribble Glass of Hair Color. And the joke's on you.

spend hours setting, combing, pinning, sculpting, spraying, and adding that last little fillip of gel, employing octopuslike skills and rubbing their necks to relieve the advanced case of cramps they've developed from craning to see the back of their own heads.

Let's just start with the subject of blow-drying. Sure, we like to think of the hours and hours that our mothers spent in beauty parlors under steel hoods as something from the Stone Age of vanity, but what's really so different about the twenty, forty, or even sixty minutes of elaborate blow-drying to force your hair into submission? Of course, when your beautician does it, it always comes out perfect. At home, it's a different story. Some women—the ones who choose not to believe that the electromagnetic waves emitted from their favorite hair tool cause brain tumors—are deeply committed to the blow-drying lifestyle.

No two blow-drying techniques are the same. Some swear that the hair must be dripping wet to start with; others insist that it be towel-dried; still others put it in a ponytail to sleep in, then wake up and blow. Another insists on a

ponytail that must be set and blow-dried at three different an-
gles, held by a banana clip. But wait, there's more. There's the
burning controversy over whether or not to use the "cold" button.
There are nozzlelike attachments to aim at only a small area of
hair at a time. You can become involved with a freakish assort-
ment of torture-implementlike brushes, long-finger diffusers, eu-
rostyling diffusers. There are those who insist that the hair must
be separated into dozens of sections and pulled severely—tension
being everything—in order to attain perfect straightness. Believe
it or not, there are women who actually enjoy this. Says one, "I use
it as time to organize my life. It's a Zen thing." Says another, "It's
like the satisfaction you get from vacuuming." And we all know
how good *that* feels.

Whether it's home haircuts, dye jobs, or Toni home perms,
the communal hair shindig is always more fun. Three girlfriends
of ours have, for years, gotten together every sixty days or so for
what they call a "henna party." It's all about getting bombed and
slapping the mudlike substance on one another's heads. This
done, shower caps are donned, then topped with elaborate, silly
hats that they sculpt from aluminum foil (this being the sum total of their art school training) to hold in the heat. It takes about
three hours to "set" the color into their hair. Already, they're

starving. Who can wait for a pizza delivery? Bickering over who'll go out to get the food, they finally all pile into the car in their wacky aluminum headgear and head for their favorite Chinese restaurant. In a sort of nineties *I Love Lucy* tableau, they blithely sweep past shocked diners and puzzled immigrant waiters, pick up their food, and return to the house to eat, drink some more, and gossip. When the timer goes off, they take turns rinsing their heads under the kitchen sink while the other two help scrub the mud out. And then, voilà! Beautiful red hair. Youth returns.

Where Angels Dare to Tread: People Who Cut Their Own Hair

A leap of faith, nerves of steel, sheer gumption, or stupidity? Whatever it takes for the untrained to cut their own hair, the people we know who do so have an amazingly cavalier attitude toward the whole thing. Says one friend, "You just have to have

faith that even if you screw up, your hair will grow back.

Our friend Al describes how she trims her split ends. Standing over her bathroom sink, she takes a section of hair, trims the ends, and then, lacking hair clips, transfers it to a "holding area"—her mouth—to separate the already-clipped hair from the still-riddled-with-split-ends hair. This works fine unless her cat comes in and uses the litter box, raising a stink she can't avoid, since she's got a mouthful of hair and is forced to breathe through her nose. This isn't the first time Al has employed flawed grooming techniques. She used to try to touch up her dark roots with bleach on a toothbrush, before dark roots were trendy, using a hand mirror for the back and the top of her head. She complains that always having her arms raised was exhausting. "Finally," she says, "I met some queen who wanted to do hair, so I'd buy a six-pack, some smokes, and go to his place. We'd gossip, drink, and smoke and he'd do the roots. God, the way it should be!"

BEAUTY INDOCTRINATION

Inherent in our baggage from childhood are memories of having to hang out for hours at the beauty parlor with Mom. This pink refuge was made up almost exclusively of robe-and-tunic-clad women who confessed their darkest secrets and their deepest fears. Gossip was exchanged, stories told, conferences held, advice and creme rinse dispensed. The women read *True Confessions*, smoked cigarettes, and sometimes ate little sandwiches while sitting under mammoth dryer hoods, waiting like cocooned worms to metamorphize into butterflies. But any girl who was forced to stay in this place with her mother, grandmother, or aunt for the entire two, three,four, five-hour duration was a girl marked for life. Bored to tears or mesmerized, the Trip to Beautiful had to rub off somehow.

CHAPTER TWO

The Trip to Beautiful

Only Your Hairdresser/Hairstylist/
Beautician/Beauty Operator/Cosmetologist/
Coiffeur/Glamour Technician Knows for Sure

THE HAIRDRESSER'S
COMMANDMENT:

It's Always about You

There's something about a visit to the salon that brings out the gabby in even the most tight-lipped. After all, the first thing they do is put that cape over your shoulders. Presto! Your body disappears from view. You're just a head, floating in space, babbling happily about your impending transformation. Your hairdresser starts by touching *your* head, feeling *your* hair, and talking to *you* about what *you* want, how *you* want to look, what style would flatter *your* features best. It's all about *you, you, you*. Plus, in between talking about your favorite subject, you get to read fashion magazines, analyze the sex life of the stars, and someone brings you beverages. It involves all the most selfish aspects of adolescence—complete license to think only of yourself, with the  oblivious assumption that those around you are just as interested.

Who is interested? The only person on earth who could possibly be as interested in how you look as you are, and who is even licensed to do something about it, is your hairdresser. What could be better than someone stroking your head and asking you what you want? Your mother is the only other person on earth who's going to do that, but all she thinks about your hair is that you should get it out of your eyes.

Is it any wonder that you spill your guts to someone whose only real job is to groom you like a poodle? The ideal situation, in my estimation, would be for all Catholic priests to get their cosmetologists' licenses and hang out a shingle advertising a confession and a cut for twenty dollars. A paternal pat on the shoulder

Beauty School Dropout

- - - - - - - -

Our friend George, a failed beautician but a successful television writer, may have had what could be called a classical beauty school training. He was inspired by the sudden hairstyling explosion of the early seventies. "This was, you'll recall, when everyone changed from the hippie look, or the still-haven't-picked-a-look-look to those perfect David Cassidy shags," says George, who was sure he could make a good living as a beauty operator while pursuing his dream of acting. So, in 1972, he enrolled at the Bensonhurst Beauty Academy in Bensonhurst, Brooklyn, and was assigned a smock, beauty supplies, and a head. (This is the unprotesting rubber mannequin head with hair that all beauty students torture down to a nub before they are allowed to do the same to beauty college clients.)

The Bensonhurst Beauty Academy (soon it would change its name to the far classier Ultissima Beauty Institute) was situated above street level on Bay Parkway in the heart of Bensonhurst. Actually featured in some shots in the film *Saturday Night Fever*, the school was a magnet for young Brooklynites with a styling comb and a dream. Says George, "We'd be disco-ing all night 'til four A.M., doing Seconals, and then we'd drag ourselves in at nine in the morning. Here's the routine: You'd smoke, gab, and s-l-o-w-l-y put rollers in your head. Or practice finger waves, which was so archaic. I mean, Bernadette Peters was maybe the only person left on earth with a finger wave. Anyway, it wasn't a big deal how it came out. You never were failed, it was all just an accumulation of hours before you could get your license. It was, in fact, only slightly stricter than the post office, where I worked at night."

When they finally let George out of the back room of the academy and onto the floor to do real live clients, he discovered he had a fatal character flaw. "I couldn't stand touching people's crusty old heads," says George, bluntly. "This was back when women would get their hair done in these rigid, durable dos once a week, and they would never wash it in between. I mean, it was disgusting! These old ladies would come in for a two-dollar haircut and they'd all want petals [the name for a particular kind of curl] with the, like, thirty-five hairs they had left on their heads!" George adds, "I only had the vaguest idea of how to cut hair, but I could do these big beautiful dos. Except, for some reason, I could only do the fronts. These old ladies would leave, all happy, tip me a big fifteen cents, and Cher—she was this girl with long black hair like Cher with a big skunk stripe running down it—Cher would see the rat's nest I had left in the back, and she'd mouth, 'That poor old thing!' It was fun to pretend to be a hairdresser, but I guess I just didn't have it in me."

from Father Murphy and you'd leap, transformed spiritually and physically, out of God's chair. "Say ten Hail Marys and please use a conditioner," he'd advise. Well . . . maybe in a more perfect world.

The most wonderful thing about hairdressers is that they all have magnificent egos. In a world of indecisive, insecure, whiney, wimpy people like ourselves, it's nice to meet people so self-assured. Most hairdressers believe they are on a mission from God to redeem your bad hair. Whether or not they disgustedly ask "who cut your hair last?" they're definitely thinking it. Deep down, they believe that they and only they are channeling the goddess of hair, and all others are fakes, charlatans, mere tacky vo-tech dropouts. It feels good to put yourself in the hands of a glamour mentor. It makes us feel secure to trust our hair to someone who, when asked how they are, says, "Livin' life and lovin it!" Who else would talk to you that way?

A good hairdresser is a good listener, intuitive enough to translate our inarticulate mumblings for "bigger on top," or "not so poufy," or "longer, but shorter" into something concrete and visible, then gently talk us out of it in favor of something more suited to our hair and our faces. A great stylist is a true artist who can see the aura of your perfect hairdo hovering invisibly just beyond your scalp.

Rudimentary haircutting skill aside, one thing all hairdressers must be able to do is listen, or at least *pretend* to. One of the biggest complaints of hairdressers is that listening to people's problems is incredibly draining, so here's the conceit: They pretend to listen to your problems, and you pretend you'll take their advice. That advice, like that given by psychiatrists and psychics alike, is given to generalities and commonsense platitudes that could apply to anyone at any time. Of course, this is just the kind of thing that makes many people believe their hairdresser to be the wisest person they know, and if they actually followed their advice, their problems might conceivably be solved.

Whatever you tell them, don't wait for a big reaction. Hairdressers are like bartenders. They've seen it all. Nothing surprises them. What's so great is that they're *still* interested. Not only that, but they are, surprisingly, great secret-keepers. And why not? It's in their best interest not to tell what they've heard in strictest confidence. They want to keep their customers.

"Tell me the most outrageous thing anyone has ever told you," I begged Myron, the man who made me a redhead.

"Oh, you know," he said in a monotone as he snipped away at my head, "the husband comes in and lets on he's cheating on the wife. Then the wife comes in and tells you she's playing around too. Then they send their boyfriends and girlfriends to you and you find out they're two-timing them too. And then there's all the plastic surgery, the sudden switches in sexual preferences, the S

Hairdresser Quiz IF YOUR BEAUTICIAN ISN'T THAT GOOD AT CUTTING HAIR, WEIGH THE ALTERNATIVES...	YES	NO
"Juicy" Gossip		
THEN I SAID, "DON'T POINT THAT THING AT ME." Fascinating Stories		
TRAGIC PAST		
EVA GABOR STARTED OUT AS AN ICE SKATER. Knowledge of... OBSCURE TRIVIA		
RESTRAINING ORDER SEX CHANGE PAROLE REHAB SWAT TEAM Bizarre Personal Life		
Amusing Attitude		

and M stuff, the corporate executive bedwetters, the client who suspects her boyfriend is a transsexual *and* a serial killer . . . just the usual kind of thing. After a while it all gets to be the same."

"Really," I said, trying not to be impressed. "But does anything in particular stick in your mind?"

"Well, this client was all excited about her new fiancé. Starts telling me what a great guy he is, blah, blah, blah. Then all of a sudden, she says, all perky, 'And guess what!' as though she's going to say, 'He has a Ferrari!' or 'He has a place at the beach!' She says, 'He has a fetish!' "He actually has to get on a plane and fly home, two thousand miles away, to satisfy this fetish." He stopped abruptly.

"What was it?" I asked.

"No," he said, "it's too specific. If I told you and it wound up in your book, she would know I told you."

"Oh, come on," I said. "No one's even going to read my book." I paused briefly as this sunk in, but then curiosity distracted me. "What IS it!?"

Myron rolled his eyes and sighed, mildly annoyed. "Oh, just say he did it with a sheep."

This only served to annoy me. "Myron, everyone knows about sex with sheep. Sex with sheep is a cliché. This must be something really juicy and bizarre. Come on!" I whined.

Myron shook his head nobly. "It is. But, sorry. Can't."

I regarded him with newfound admiration. "Wow," I said. "Ethical. Cool." My mind was a whirlwind of sick ideas.

LIFESTYLES OF THE BOLD AND THE BEAUTIFUL

If you are someone who prefers not to talk about yourself, and you don't care to hear about your hairdresser's other clients, he or she can probably entertain you with stories about his or her own colorful existence. I'm not saying that all hairdressers are wild, party-seeking, multiple-divorcées in whose handbags there can always be found a bottle of vodka, a bag of pain pills, and a gun. Let's just say that this glamour-oriented profession is a magnet for *excitement*.

Do all hairdressers, no matter how settled down and domestic, have bad boyfriends, large bar tabs, irate landlords, irksome cars, IRS trouble, positive urine tests, negative bank accounts and unlicensed handguns? Well, of course not. Some of them have the smug satisfaction of knowing that at least they're not as screwed up as you. And even if they are, at least their hair is always going to look good.

One Hairdresser's Bizarre Personal Life

A friend of mine was getting her hair done for a while by a guy who was an overweight Austrian with a platinum flattop, an outrageous Colonel Klink accent and an incredible array of bizarre family stories. His haircutting was pretty good, but his family anecdotes were to die for.

"So, Hans, was your family in Austria during the war?"

"Yah, did I ever tell you about how my grandmutter vas raped in da mountain pass by soldiers?"

"Oh, that's terrible. The Nazis?"

"No. Ve vere de Nazis."

CURL UP AND DYE:

Cellophaning, Green Hair, Oxidation, and Other Hair-Coloring Mysteries

All hairdressers seem to agree: The color they can give you is better than any color found in nature. Hair coloring is an art and an inexact science, at best. Most hairdressers will tell you that the only time problems arise is when a client isn't being truthful about the hair products they've been using. The clients are intim-

Lines Hairdressers Use to Cover Their Mistakes

"I LIKE IT BETTER
THIS WAY."

"IT LOOKS SO MUCH
BETTER THAN IT DID
WHEN YOU CAME IN."

"I'M TRYING SOMETHING
NEW, AND YOU'RE THE
VERY FIRST!"

"NOW, THIS PERM
IS GOING TO RELAX
IN JUST A FEW DAYS."

"IF WE COLOR IT
AGAIN, ALL YOUR
HAIR WILL FALL OUT."

"WELL, YOU'RE GROWING
IT AND WE NEED TO KEEP
IT THE RIGHT SHAPE."

"ALL THE BIG MODELS ARE
WEARING IT THIS WAY."

"YOU LOOK JUST LIKE
DENNIS RODMAN."

"IT'LL TONE
DOWN."

idated by the salon colorist and may be afraid to confess that they've been seeing another bottle, or maybe even another hairdresser, on the side. Mix and match your chemicals, and your head could turn into one big bubbling test tube. Women have been known to spend entire days in salons as the whole staff tries to perform the delicate task of coloring, stripping color, reapplying more color. Scalps are seared. Husbands call repeatedly and are told, darkly, "She can't come to the phone." More nightmares, more stripping, hair falls out in clumps or turns to a florescent mush. Finally, she staggers into the twilight, transformed into an interesting little ochre pixie of a woman.

SALON VERSUS BEAUTY PARLOR

I have a friend who insists on calling the hair place she frequents "the beauty parlor," just to rankle the stylists, whom she refers to as "the beauty operators." I like "beauty operators" too. It sounds like all they have to do is connect you with the right hairstyle, and then you're talkin' beauty! Our moms went to the beauty parlor. We go to the salon. As in, "It looks like you just stepped out of a salon!" A beauty parlor is a cosier place where women chain-smoked and cracked gum and read *True Confessions* and put their ped-clad feet up while under the fleshy-colored permanent wave machine. The beauty operators were all sassy, maternal, wise-cracking types, the waitresses of the hair world. Now when a severe foreign man with a thick accent cuts and blow-dries your hair with the concentration of a monk raking a Zen rock garden, you leave chic but spiritually empty.

The hair salon withholds its approval, disdaining you as a "before," finding you suitable only as an "after." The beauty parlor, on the other hand, is a temple of hope, a place rife with life-changing possibilities—and the pipeline to really juicy gossip. Here you

can absorb glamour, bond with your friends, dish your head off, and get that *entre nous*, doing-drugs-in-the-bathroom-feeling without the annoying side effects, and you are physically transformed. You leave looking better than you did when you came in. A beauty parlor is where everybody knows your name; *Cheers* without the liver damage.

SILLY SALON NAMES FROM COAST TO COAST

The bottom line of cutting hair may be business, but that doesn't mean the business names have to be serious. Certain name trends prevail, coast to coast. Hairdressers apparently think they're on to something original with endless duplications of weak wordplay involving "cut," "hair," "shear," and "mane." Of course, the hallmark of small business is alliterations, and in the case of beauty salons, *K*'s standing in for *C*'s. Most of all, there's French—well, the Pepe LePew version of French, anyway. There's also a reason they became hairdressers instead of English teachers.

Cumulatively, these names represent a form of poetry, a vision of the aspirations of people who give their lives to hair. I imagine hearing these names, as spoken repeatedly by regionally accented, lipglossed receptionists, in southern twang or Baltimore nasal honk, midwestern flat vowels or Western sharp consonants, as they answer the phones in the windows in small shops in small towns, in large salons in big cities.

"Questionable Imagery"

Headhunters-
   Tulsa, OK
Head Locks-Waco, TX
Blockhead-Houston, TX
Dar's Hair Chair-
   Inwood, IA
Hair Hut-numerous
   Hair Kingdom-
      Baltimore, MD
   Afro Hut Unlimited-
      Baltimore, MD
Another Bad Creation-
   Baltimore, MD
Better Now Than Later-
   Baltimore, MD
Hairobics-Dallas, TX

City of Hair-San Antonio, TX
A Hairy Situation-numerous
Big Hairy Deal-Le Seuer, MN
Butch and Hairy's Salon -
   Queensbury, NY
Hairy Spot - Escanaba, MI
The Hairy Ape Hair Designers-
   Coral Gables, FL
The Hairy Cactus Salon -
   Cincinnati, OH
Can Doo - Centralia, WA
Shuns Styles -
   Oklahoma City, OK
Nail It To Me - Minneapolis, MN
Crazy Scissors - Dallas, TX
Studio 911 - Houston, TX

Tangles - Hugo, OK

Ali Baba Cave of Beauty -
    Opa-Locka, FL

Alamo Scratch - Alamo, CA

Alley Cats Hair Shop -
    Muncy, PA

Shear Dye-Nasty -
    Baltimore, MD

Cowcutta's Hair Salon -
    Amarillo, TX

Bushwacker's Beauty Salon -
    Morrilton, AR

Spoiled Rotten - Prescott, AR

Poor Boy & Gal -
    Lockesburg, AR

1 Bad Kut Hair & Nail Salon -
    Ocala, FL

OK Beauty Salon - Detroit, MI

Mandingo & Hair Breeding -
    Newark, NJ

Kaboom Hair Salon -
    Middleton, WI

Hair Explosion -
    Baltimore, MD

Beauty Bush - several

Shape Rat & Roll - Tulsa, OK

Wapoo Cuts - Charleston, SC

Waterless Technology -
    North Pole, AK

Little Bit of Country -
    Hugo, OK

Sherry's Hair
    Corral - Garrison, TX

Irma's Beauty Barn -
    Nacodoches, TX

Cotton Patch Family Styling -
    Tulsa, OK

Country Curl - Gonzales, TX

Wood on Western -
    Oklahoma City, OK

Becky & Dot's Beauty Shop -
Tulsa, OK

Vernola's House of Beauty -
Oklahoma City, OK

Juanita's Cut-n-Curl -
Oklahoma City, OK

Etha Lee Collins Beauty Nook -
Fort Worth, TX

Beehive Full Service
Salon - Honey
Grove, TX

Hazel's Hair Fashions -
Fort Worth, TX

Lady Louise's Beauty Bar -
Waco, TX

Shirl's Curls - Midland, TX

Pamper Me Please -
Midland, TX

Beauty Booth - Lubbock, TX

Jo-Lynn Beauty Den -
Midland, TX

Jackie's Hair Flair -
Schulenberg, TX

Bobbie Nell's Beauty Salon -
Gonzales, TX

Berna's Beauty Place -
Morrilton, AR

Bon-Ette Beauty Salon -
Malvern, AR

Queen Bee - Malvern, AR

Dot's Looking Glass - Hope, AR

Queenie's Beauty Box -
Anchorage, AK

Wanita's Ladybug - Sparta, NJ

A Beautiful Eyedea -
Baton Rouge, LA

A Touche of Class
- Newark, DE

Be Lov Lee Beauty
Shop - San Antonio, TX

Shur Kut - Houston, TX

Pa-Zazz Hair Salon - numerous

Capelli Hair Dizine - Odessa, TX

Hair Dimention - Victoria, TX

Hair D-Zires Studio -
    Baltimore, MD

Phaz 1 Hair Design- Victoria, TX

Phaze Uno - Baltimore, MD

Powdour Pouf Beauty Salon -
    Minneapolis, MN

Jazze Styles - Baltimore, MD

Short Cutz - Baltimore, MD

Renaiss Art Salon -
    Rockville Centre, NY

Hair Dinamics - Lynbrook, NY

"J"ust Renea's -
    Greenville, TN

'N'Dulge - El Paso, TX

'N'Styl - Baker, MT

Ka-Ris'ma - Harrison, ME

Kadee's Lords and Ladees -
    Pittsburgh, PA

Kair About Hair -
    Cincinnati, OH

Kajun Kutz - Plaquemine, LA

Kalifornia Styl Hair and Nails -
    Dallas, TX

Kar-4-U Nails and Hair -
    Norco, CA

Kar-a-Cel Hair Design Inc. -
    Roselle, IL

Kar-Fre Hair Design -
    Danese, WV

Kabin Kuts - Talkeethna, AK

Kandy's Korner Kut -
    Corning, CA

Katrina's Kreations -
    Lubbock, TX

Kay's Klip & Kurl Salon -
    Malvern, AR

K's Kurl Kottage - La Crosse, KS

Kim's Kutting Korral - Bogota, TX

KK's Cut Ups - Malvern, AR

Kae's Kountry Kurl - Hebron, MD

Krazy Kuts - Amarillo, TX

Kreative Klippers - Lubbock, TX

Kutting Korner Beauty Shop -
    Telephone, TX

Kutting Krew - Hot Springs, AR

Sassy Scissors Salon -
    Malvern, AR

Suds & Scissors
Hairstyling -
Malvern, AR

Terrific Tom of Amarillo -
    Amarillo, TX

A+B Hairporium - Clinton, IL

Hair We Are - numerous

"Hair" Azona - Sioux Falls, SD

Hair Port - numerous

Hair's the Place - numerous

Hair It Tizz - numerous

Hair's Patti - Yorktown, TX

Hair's To You - numerous

Hair's Our Place -
    numerous

Hairmaster - numerous

Hairsations -
    Lyndhurst, NJ

Biggest Little Hairhouse
    - numerous

Delta Hairlines -
    Nashville, AR

Laws of Hair - Baldwin, NY

JJ's Syndicut - Nacodoches, TX

Little Sahaira's - Lubbock, TX

Just Cuttin-Up - Flatonia, TX

Total-E-Clips - Victoria, TX

Bobby Shop - Amarillo, TX

Judy's Swing N Set -
    Morrilton, AR

La Moor Beauty Salon -
    Oklahoma City, OK

A'Mor Hair and Nail
    Salon - Odessa, TX

A La Scherie -numerous

Lamartinique -
    Detroit, MI

Afri-Tique Unisex Salon -
    several
De Ja Vue - Oklahoma City, OK
Vu Ja De Designer Cuts -
    Amarillo, TX
Jo-La-Ru Beauty Salon -
    Conway, AR
"Ah" La Feet Face and Hands -
    Stafford, TX
Kiki La Chelles -
    Oklahoma City, OK
Flor De Liz Beauty Salon -
    Odessa, TX
Salon Nuvo - Fort Worth, TX
Hairtique - Baldwin, NY
Emile Hairniques -
    Baltimore, MD
Tress Chic - Amarillo, TX
Hair Classique by Wanda
    and Mary - Hampstead, NY
Coiffures by Le Gloria -
    Dallas, TX

Reflections of Ducharme -
    Paris, TX
Jaque's Fashionette Salon -
    Gonzales, TX
L'Better For Hair -
    Maineville, OH
L'Pearl Design - Abilene, TX
L'Elegantly U - Detroit, MI
La Beautee Chez Pamela -
    Tempe, AZ

La Casa de la Belle - Bronx, NY
La Chateau de Glamour -
    Philadelphia, PA
La Perfecto Salon -
    Fort Worth, TX
La Delisia Beauty Shop -
    Fort Worth, TX

Lady Di Beauty Salon - Dallas, TX

Royal Headquarters - Royal, AR

Hair Majesty - San Antonio, TX

Lord's & Lady's -

   Rockville Centre, NY

Shirley's Foxy Lady - Detroit, MI

L'il Bit of Class - Paris, TX

A Classy Lady - Las Vegas, NV

Master Pieces - Bogota, TX

Styles Ga-Lore -

   Nacodoches, TX

Hi-Hat Beauty Shop -

   Fort Worth, TX

Artistic Beauty Shop -

   Fort Worth, TX

Charme Shoppe - Yoakum, TX

A Touch of Paris Coiffure -

   Baltimore, MD

Karen and Glenda's Glam-

   ourama - Wiggins, MS

J-Su's House Of Hair - Lufkin, TX

Disciples Village - Tulsa, OK

Hair Blessing - Baltimore, MD

Jucas Higher Creation Beauty

   Studio - Philadelphia, PA

Mr. J Golden Buddha Beauty

   Salon - Franklin, IN

Sufi & Sufi International Hair

   Studio - Houston, TX

Jesus Cares Beauty Salon -

   Huntsville, AL

Who Done It - Jesus - Chicago, IL

Jesus Christ & Us -

    Daytona Beach, FL

Sacred Well - Whitethorn, CA

Glory To God Salon -

    Saint Matthews, SC

God's Anointed Hair Designs -

    Austin, TX

God's Elect Hair Designers -

    Kenner, LA

God's Miracle Christian Beauty

    Salon - Crescent City, FL

Thank God I'm Beautiful -

    Roy, UT

LITERARY REFERENCES

East of Eden - Dallas, TX

A Room With a Do -

    Wichita, KS

Vanity Flair - Gonzales, TX

From Hair to Eternity -

    numerous

Doll's House - numerous

Out of Africa - numerous

Scarlett O'Haira's -

    numerous

HAIR RULE NUMBER THREE: *There are no bad hairdressers —just women who won't obey their instincts.*

JUST BECAUSE MY HAIR IS FUSCHIA DOESN'T MEAN YOURS WILL BE TOO

Contrary to popular belief, the wacky hairdressers with the constantly changing hair color and style are not necessarily to be avoided. In fact, they are noble, self-sacrificing artists ever in search of innovation. Like the scientist who first tries a new serum on him or herself, they would rather suffer the effects of an experiment gone wrong than to harm a hair on anyone else's head. Just don't necessarily follow their advice about your love life.

Hairdressers Who've Gone On to Bigger Things

Danny DeVito, Ringo Starr, Fran Drescher, Jon Peters, Bugs Bunny, Debi Mazar, Chuck Berry, George Clinton, Tammy Wynette

Why Getting Your Hair Done is Better Than Psychiatry

		THERAPIST	HAIRDRESSER	
	INTERESTED IN HEARING ABOUT YOUR MOTHER	X	X	
	ASKS ABOUT YOUR LOVE LIFE	X	X	
	TEDIOUS PROBING ABOUT FAILED RELATIONSHIPS	X		
	REALLY UNDERSTANDS YOUR SUBCONSCIOUS NEEDS		X	
	POO-POOS ASTROLOGY	X		
	KNOWS A GOOD PSYCHIC		X	
	AGREES A NEW HAIRSTYLE COULD CHANGE YOUR LIFE		X	
	ANNOYING INSISTENCE THAT YOU CONFRONT YOUR PROBLEMS	X		
	BRINGS YOU TO TEARS ON A REGULAR BASIS	X		
	DOESN'T BELIEVE IN ANTIDEPRESSANTS	X		
	HAS VALIUM IN PURSE		X	

		THERAPIST	HAIRDRESSER
	WILL DISCUSS OTHER CLIENTS		X
	WILL DISCUSS COLORFUL PAST		X
	OPTION OF WAXING UPPER LIP		X
	VESTED INTEREST IN YOUR APPEARANCE		X
	WILL MASSAGE YOUR SCALP		X
	TELLS YOU THE TRUTH ABOUT HOW YOU LOOK		X
	SUBSCRIBES TO VOGUE		X
	WILL TELL YOU ABOUT THEIR SEX LIFE		X
	ASKS "HOW DO YOU FEEL ABOUT IT?"	X	X
	KNOWS ABOUT HAIR CARE PRODUCTS		X
	ANALYZES YOUR DREAMS	X	X
	WOULD BE FUN TO GO TO VEGAS WITH		X
	EXPECTS A TIP		X

CHAPTER THREE

Modern Hair History

Shock Value: Hair as Political Statement, or Fifty Ways to Bug Your Mother

~~It used to be~~ ~~all you had to do was~~ grow your hair long and ~~you could infuriate~~ anyone ~~over~~ thirty. These days, it takes a little ~~more imagination.~~ Despite the fact that fashion-forward grand-mothers use Crazy Color, fifty-year-old white supremacists sport waist-length hair, and everyone, it seems, is shaving his or her head, there will always be a new hair frontier to cross. This is be-cause children are born with the instinctive knowledge that they can use their hair to piss off their parents. Extreme hair is a uni-versal coming-of-age rite.

TV FULL OF HAIR

Not only is TV responsible for all modern hair, it's safe to say that in TV land, hair is a major obsession. Since the 1950s we've been able to study idealized hair on a daily basis. Did the Beatles really jump-

start the counterculture? Were they really the ones responsible for a generation of peace and love? Think again. Get ready for HAIR RULE NUMBER FOUR: *Captain Kangaroo was the first freak.* He was there first, subliminally sending the message to children under the age of ten that long hair was cool. And perhaps the phrase "tune in, turn on, and drop out" was really about watching TV for clues on what to do with all this new hair.

From there, the hair floodgates opened. Peggy Lipton in *Mod Squad*, Maureen McCormick in *The Brady Bunch*, and Susan Dey in *The Partridge Family* all shared one thing—that perfectly straight, satin curtain of hair that all adolescent girls so desperately wanted that swung from side to side when you walked. Marlo Thomas's perky flip in *That Girl*, Loni Anderson's bizarre bouffant meltdown from *WKRP*, and, of course, Farrah Fawcett's hair—the hair that shaped a nation—all are burned into our collective unconscious. And it's not just the gals. Think of Kookie and his comb from *77 Sunset Strip*, the boyish Illya Kuryakin's *Man from U.N.C.L.E.* moptop, Steve McGarrett's tsunami pompadour in *Hawaii Five-o*, and David

Cassidy's *Partridge Family* shag. They all made it look so easy—and this was before the innocent, unwashed public even knew exactly how they were supposed to manage all this hair, in a pre–blow-dryer era. Who knew these TV stars had an army of hairdressers working double overtime?

Today, with a hundred channels and more, your television set is a twenty-four-hour, complete, up-to-the-second encyclopedia of hair. Channel surf and revisit vintage TV hairdos. Keep up with the current state of evangelists' (always big) hair. Study the rugs and plugs of your favorite stars on shows like *Entertainment Tonight.* Music videos are your best bet for current extreme coifs. Compare and contrast the soap opera hair of American stars versus their Latino and Asian counterparts. Marvel at classic eighties Big Hair on reruns of *Dallas* and *Dynasty.* The worst hair on TV?

The Evolution of the Farrah Hairdo

| 1977: FARRAH, HAIR ROLE MODEL | 1981: WENDY, FLIGHT ATTENDANT | 1984: SHANELLE, UNEM- PLOYED | 1987: DEBBIE, CLAIMS ADJUSTOR | 1990: SHANIQUA, MANAGER | 1993: ANGIE, GANG GIRL | 1996: HOWARD, RADIO PER- SONALITY |

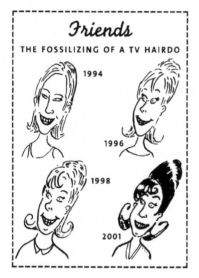

Friends
THE FOSSILIZING OF A TV HAIRDO
1994
1996
1998
2001

The tresses of the guests of daytime talk shows.

Garry Shandling has made a permanent case for hair neurosis on television. *Seinfeld*'s Kramer has already made hair history. *Friends*'s Jennifer Aniston's earthshaking ur-shag, the Farrah do of the nineties, captured America's hair imagination. It continues to mutate, just as Farrah's did and does. In fact, after the *Friends* hairdo, it seemed every other female star and newscaster on network or cable was sporting a copycat shaggy flip.

Newscaster Hair

Is it sexist to pick on women newscasters for their helmet hair? Absolutely. For one thing, the air has finally been let out of those network news dos. These days, they're all sporting those sleek, soignée, little pixies that stay in the background rather than scream for attention. The men, on the other hand . . . well, let's talk about the men. Ted Koppel's going for that Kennedy wedge, but it just looks like he glued his mom's mink collar to his forehead. Tom Brokaw is pushing the outside of the hair envelope with a deep, deep side part. Sam Donaldson makes too much money to have a toupee that bad. Message to Sam: What's with the Spock eyebrows? And Dan Rather: What's the frequency, Kenneth?

Barbara Walters is in a class all by herself. Always one step ahead of her hair critics, Babs changes her do more often than many of us change our underwear. But maybe it's just to take our minds off the speech impediment. She is a Big Hair Gal (see chapter four) of her own free will. Likewise Maria Shriver. Anyone who's

NETWORK ANCHOR HAIR

REGIONAL NEWSCASTER HAIR

kin to Jackie Onassis *and* married to Arnold Schwarzenegger has no choice. Diane Sawyer? She's a blonde. 'Nuff said. Jane Pauley, on the other hand, is the real hair pioneer. No woman married to a political satirist could ever be a Big Hair Gal. If you look back at Jane over the years, you can tell she's been fighting for a long time to gain control of her on-screen coif. Sure, Katie, Joan, the whole lot of them can just wash it and go because Jane was there first.

Who, exactly, are the people who make decisions about the way regional news reporters wear their hair? Do the producers think a big, inflated back-combed flip the texture of cold toast with a skunk stripe running through it will distract us from all those senseless shootings, city hall scandals, and murder-suicides? Or do they think the female audience tunes in just to see what Kristy, Judy, or Lauren is doing with her hair today? Just look at their male counterparts. You could hardly point to sexism here when you see anchormen with Frisbee-shaped toupees; toupees that resemble Persian lamb evening bags; highly engineered combovers; flat-topped or pompadoured sportscasters; and those ever-tanned, ever-peppy weathermen with *Saturday Night Fever* blow-dried dos. The infotainment needs to be taken out of the news copy and put on top of the heads of the newscasters, where it belongs.

F I L M : *The Subject Was Hair*

Shampoo, right. *Hairspray*, duh. *Steel Magnolias*, yeah, yeah. *Hair*. Right. But there are a lot of movies out there that are more about hair than you would think. The general rule of thumb for a hair movie is when you spend more time thinking about the actors' hair than you do listening to the dialogue.

The Women

An entire story of marital infidelity hinges on the offhand remark made by a blabby manicurist in a beauty parlor, where saintly doormat wife Norma Shearer learns that she and bitchy Saks clerk Joan Crawford share not only the same nail polish (Jungle Red!) but the same man.

The Last of the Mohicans

In the battle of the hairdos, Daniel Day-Lewis and Madeleine Stowe compete for prettiest tresses while fighting off the guys who invented the Mohawk.

Legends of the Fall

One good brother, one bad, and one with bouncin' and behavin' hair.

Splash

Not so much a mermaid movie as a film about logistically placed hair over Daryl Hannah's chest.

Klute

This film from 1971 without question kicked off the shag era. Sure, you could call it a terse detective story. I call it a 114-minute hairdo commercial.

Dances with Wolves

All many people can think about through the whole movie is how white-girl-raised-by-Native-Americans Mary McDonnell happens to have a perfect seventies' shag when all her Indian stepsisters have hair down to their asses.

Prince of Tides

Oh my gawd. Barbra's haih. Like buttah. Likewise the nails. The story? Who caehs?

Braveheart

The one detail Mel Gibson couldn't work into the script? How twelfth century Scot martyr William Wallace invented mousse, dreadlocks, and extensions. Now, that's what I call a hero.

It Could Happen to You

Rosie Perez is supposed to prove that all hairdressers are nasty, tacky, greedy, shallow, insensitive bitches when she plays the beautiful, ambitious, and outspoken beauty-operator wife who fails to understand why big-hearted New York City cop hubby Nicolas Cage would want to give half of his $2 million Lotto ticket as a tip to drippy blond waitress Bridget Fonda, who's supposedly nicer and has "better" taste than his wife.

Working Girl

A great study of truly, wonderfully bad office-worker hair. By the time Melanie Griffith gets her overmoussed do chopped off, you're rooting for Joan Cusack's character to stab her with the scissors and be done with it all.

Valley of the Dolls

Bitchy Patty Duke throws bitchier Susan Hayward's wig into the potty. Hilarity ensues.

Presumed Innocent

Harrison Ford donned a "Caesar" do for this 1991 movie, but since this style is really nothing more than a forward combover, they should've called it "Presumed Bald."

Showgirls

This movie, the absolute Mount Olympus of high camp, is a paean to vulgarity and silly hair. Wigs, blondness, and trashy tresses abound, but my favorite do in the whole movie is showgirl-screwing casino exec Kyle MacLachlan's unlikely junior high school Beatle-style moptop, which makes him look less like a swinging bachelor than it does a ninth-grade class president with Gary and the Playboys delusions.

The Lion King

All Disney animated features are about big hair, since every action figure and doll modelled on the cartoon characters must have it in abundance. But in *The Lion King*, Simba's mane is completely over the top. When he reaches young lionhood, his tousled tresses resemble those of none other than vintage Jon Bon Jovi. Throwing a very un-Disneyish kink into things, the lionesses put us in mind of—how to put it?—sexy bald chicks.

Saturday Night Fever

This movie is a testament to the power of the blow-dryer. Ten minutes into the film, Tony Manero, disco king of Bay Ridge, Brooklyn, has already styled himself a magnificent molded dry-look pompadour. When he's backhanded at the dinner table by his father, Tony flinches, whining, "Wouldja just watch the haih!?" Turning to his mother for defense, he says, "Y'know, I worked on the haih a long time, and he hits it. He hits my haih!"

Interview with a Vampire

Tom Cruise is a blond, Brad Pitt pouts even though he has perfect hair, but poor, cute Kirsten Dunst is the only one of these vampires who is truly damned for all eternity. Try as she might, she can't unload those dopey sausage curls!

In Like Flint

This parody of sixties' spy movies features a secret society of supersexy gals with big flippy hair who plot to take over the world by brainwashing housewives with subliminal messages inside beauty shop dryer hoods!

Bad Working Hollywood Hair

Rumor had it that Howard Cosell's toupees almost had their own Saturday morning cartoon, but recently the worst showbiz hair-

piece award must go to Mr. Burt Reynolds. This, indeed, is **HAIR MYSTERY NUMBER TWO:** *If you make that much money, can't you afford a better rug?*

MUSIC HAIR

Hair sells songs. Everyone knows this. Little Richard knows it. Elvis knew it. The Beatles knew it. Hair is sexy. Hair gets attention. Hair moves to the beat. Interestingly, because rock music has been, until recently, a sexist and unwelcoming business for women musicians, the hairdos of male rock singers have had to suffice as role models for their legions of fans, male and female. Outside of trying to recreate the wigs of the Supremes, or wondering what Janis Joplin did to make her hair look so bad, this left, God-knows-how-many millions of women yearning for tresses like Donovan's, Peter Frampton's, Greg Allman's. Gosh! How *did* they get such dreamy hair?

Once, it was easy to tell a music act by its hair. Long hair—rock. Short hair meant something square, something Lawrence Welk–like. The Man. To youth, short hair was the problem, long hair the solution. These days, with the music industry exploding with all kinds of sounds, it's hard to tell who's on whose side. Poli-

tics left, right, and center have all come to recognize the importance of attractive hair, which makes defining a politician or the leader of a movement by his or her hair difficult indeed. One thing is certain. The hit machine is still hair-driven. This leads to HAIR RULE NUMBER FIVE: *The bigger the hair, the more sentimental the music.* Michael Bolton? Big Hair. Michael Jackson? Big, Gooey Hair. Celine Dion? A wig on a stick. Whether it's country or rock 'n' roll, heavy metal or pop, rap or adult contemporary, gospel or soul, you can bet by the sound of the song whether or not the singer has a big do. Let's just put it this way. The harder it is to style, the easier it is to listen to, or not. It's the Kenny Law. Kenny G, Kenny Loggins, Kenny Rogers. Big Hair. Soft, soft, silly songs.

Of course, since rock 'n' roll hair is supposed to be about rebellion, youth, and irritating people over thirty, then the downside is, of course, getting old. The Rolling Stones and Aerosmith, rock's grand old men, refuse to conform to society's standards of how they should look or act at their age. You may say, "right on, dude!" (or perhaps some other outdated phrase) but the unfortunate result is that these men are starting to look like aging B-movie actresses with too much plastic surgery who can't believe no one wants to buy them a drink. Is it worse when they're imprisoned in the amber of their old image, or when they try to keep up with the latest looks?

Whole Lotta Shakin' Goin' On: The Fifties

In no other business is hair such a critical factor as it is in rock. Acts rise and fall on the strength, body, wave, and bounce of their dos. Little Richard had to be the first, or at least the first most *famous* musician, to have the most outrageous hair in rock 'n' roll. Of course, soul and R and B performers' hair was a totally amazing and awe-inspiring cavalcade of conks, processes, and marcel waves. Elvis, of course, stole it all and made it his own—swivel hips, a black-sounding voice, and a naturally straight conk. In fact, in its day, Elvis's hair was considered long, but his was just one of many variations of the highly sculptural rockabilly coifs. Jerry Lee Lewis's wild tresses *were* long, but somehow engineered into a massive pompadour atop his head. As he'd pound out "Great Balls of Fire," it would collapse, like the fall of Rome, into his eyes.

Gimme a Head with Hair: The Sixties

The Beatles, of course, Captain Kangaroo notwithstanding, *made* hair in the sixties. Grinding out their songs for years in Hamburg dives, their break didn't come until a German girlfriend styled their trademark "moptops."[1] All through the sixties, as the Beatles' hair went, so went a nation of bands. If you were a rock 'n' roll musician and you didn't have a Beatle cut, your career was over. For God's sake, it had to be in your eyes, because this is what seemed to irritate the adults the most. The critical detail, among men, was that it wasn't supposed to be styled—that was simply too bourgeois, and too effeminate.

All the Young Dudes: The Seventies

Suddenly, in a world that had formerly trusted long hair only if it was completely unruly, it was okay for a guy to get his hair

----

1. Paul McCartney effectively invented the thing that made him irresistible to the world: the Hair Toss. Many would imitate it. None would succeed.

styled. Glam-rock and heavy metal ruled the earth, and getting the right look was labor-intensive. This gave rise to "unisex" hair salons, with men suddenly spending almost as much time on their dos as the gals.

Model-perfect David Bowie was the only person in the world capable of wearing an Afghan hound-like shag, a do that made everyone else look like an idiot (Rod Stewart and the Bay City Rollers for two). But Bowie's new, parent-annoying twist was to add plucked eyebrows, rouge, and eye shadow. Kiss went a step further with Kabuki makeup and geisha hair. Peter Frampton was the male answer to Farrah Fawcett with his big, floppy ringlets to match his "mellow rock" style.

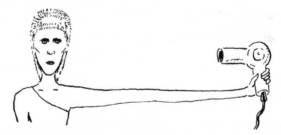

Afros reached astonishing proportions. When all five of the Jacksons sat down to chat with Mike Douglas on his talk show, there was hardly room in the camera shot for them *and* their hair! Speaking of Afros, the Average White Band, a white, Scottish

The Fros We Know

THE CATHOLIC LADY AFRO
("THE CATHFRO")

THE KOREAN PERM
("THE KOFRO")

THE HIP, SWINGIN' JEWISH AFRO
("THE HEBRO")

group, sought to completely immerse themselves in funk by sporting suspiciously unnatural nappy dos.

Disco—especially the Bee Gees—brought the Dry Look to new levels. Acres of perfectly molded floss atop the heads of Barry, Robin, and Maurice[2] gave them the appearance of being airbrushed, matching their perfect, chipmunkish harmonies. One reaction to disco was to stay firmly entrenched in hippie land. Just keep wearing your hair really, really long. Ideally, long, perfectly straight curtains of hair like Greg Allman[3], Grand Funk Railroad's Mark Farner, and Ted Nugent, were exactly what teenage boys yearned for to piss off their parents and impress girls, of course, who also wanted exactly the same hairdo.

----

2. Mid-1970s Barry Gibb is a perfect example of the art of the blow-dryer.
3. The failure of Cher's marriage to Greg Allman can be traced to Hair Rule Number Seven (see chapter five).

Finally, as a complete rejection of disco, punk brought back short hair. A delightfully refreshing display of spiky dead black or spiky dead platinum hair, or (at the time) shockingly candy-colored Mohawks, constructed, it was rumored, with Krazy Glue and always accented, of course, by safety pins through the nose. This brings up **HAIR MYSTERY NUMBER THREE:** *How do you sleep in a Mohawk?* But what about the Women of Rock? Debby Harry wowed 'em with her vacant stare and her wispy, carelessly styled platinum locks. Girls like the Runaways, Joan Jett, and Chrissie Hynde were working a tough-chick look, as only someone armed with eyeliner, a teasing comb, and a guitar could.

Haircut Bands: The Eighties

Heavy metal and glam-rock melded in the eighties to create "haircut bands," pretty boys who generally played cheesy pop songs disguised as metal. Ratt, Cinderella, and Poison, the most successful examples, sported highly styled, fried-and-dyed tresses. The style survives to this day in a fossilized form as the quintessential mall hair in places like suburban Long Island. Twisted Sister fea-

PRINCE + DAVID LEE ROTH = DEB

tured Dee Snider's blond Shirley Temple ringlets.

Another school, English New Wave, brought bands known as much for their asymmetrical, razored dos and stylized pompadours as for their synthesizer-heavy musical style. They included Flock of Seagulls, Human League, and the aptly named Haircut 100. Rock-star hair continued to build to a moussey crescendo atop the heads of people like Jon Bon Jovi, David Lee Roth, and Prince. Guns 'n' Roses featured another curtain-o-hair, Axl Rose, and their very own Cousin It in the form of guitarist Slash. Prince peeked poutily from beneath a Louis XIV pompadour. One of the biggest news headlines of the eighties was when Michael Jackson's relaxed locks, dripping with Jeri-Curl, caught on fire during the making of a Pepsi commercial. Madonna broke through as the first female megastar of the eighties with an ever-changing parade of hairstyles that firmly cemented the link between rock and fashion. The Material Girl frustrated millions of fans, because by the time they'd figure out how to get their hair like hers, she'd already moved on to a new do.

Smells Like Teen Spirit: The Nineties

The nineties saw ghetto fashion and hair still influencing rap music with cornrows, extensions, elaborate sculptural braiding, and dreadlocks. Grunge, with its thrift-store look, was responsible for bringing back flat, straight, parted-down-the-middle seventies' hair. But largely, instead of individuals exerting an effect on popular culture, the opposite is happening. The corporatization of pop music—MTV—calls for controlling the image spin. An act's look

becomes carefully contrived from demo tape to top ten video. Image consultants, stylists, and hairdressers are brought in to make over the bands. They examine street fashion, then design something similar that can be sold for lots more money at the mall. The act is "positioned" in these clothes in the video and the exact same outfits are in the stores when the video makes its debut. So these days, when you want to look like your favorite singer, is it an act of rebellion, or an act of capitalism? But don't worry. Youth will always find a new way to annoy. It's just a matter of how many seconds it takes the spin doctors to co-opt this annoyance.

Country Hair

Real country is emotionally charged. The hair's got to match. Real country divas—the ones who can sing through their noses about restraining orders, custody battles, deadbeat daddies—might temporarily trade all that height and backcombing for tasteful little shags, because they like to stay on top of things too. But when it comes down to being a woman who can make a grown man weep over a jukebox at 2 A.M., a country diva needs big hair. Her audience goes to see spangles and wigs. Dolly knows this. Tammy knew this. Loretta knows it too. They remember the days when their hairpieces required their own tour buses.

If women in country music have let us down hair-wise, lately, the men have done much worse. The hat epidemic has swept the industry, from George Strait to Garth Brooks, leaving us all wondering what's underneath. Charlie Rich, the Silver Fox, so named for his trademark silver pompadour, Conway Twitty's distinctive sideburns, even Willie Nelson's silly pigtails—these were all attention-getting hairdos. What've the men in country music done for us lately, hair-wise? Aside from Marty Stuart proving that a man can wear his hair like Reba McEntire and apparently get away with it, not a lot. But if there is one man in country music who has done more to set back the progress of American hair than everyone else combined, that man is one-hit-wonder Billy Ray Cyrus.

BAD HAIR YEARS:
Other Just Plain Bad Hairdos of Our Times

* The "could you look a little more stupid, please?" ponytail on top of the head.

* Suzanne Somers' "Chrissy Snow"–job from *Three's Company*. No self-respecting little girl would be caught wearing these ponytails.

✱ The Bo Derek cornrows: Where cornrows look extremely lovely and attractive on women with darker skin and bold features, there is something about seeing a bunch of wimpy, limp little raggedy braids hanging around the face of someone with pale skin and European features that simply shouts African-American wannabe!

The Shag Timeline . . .

OR, HOW THE SHAG CRAWLED BACK ON TOP
OF OUR HEADS AND BECAME A BOUFFANT

1972   1978   1979   1980   1983   1985   1988   1991   1993   1996

CHAPTER FOUR

Bigger-Than-Life Hair
The Woman Who Can Defy Gravity Can Do Anything

THE BIG HAIR PHILOSOPHY

Some women are born with Big Hair, and some rise to it. Others just depend on wigs. Whatever the case, it takes a certain kind of woman to carry off the Big Hair style. We call her a Big Hair Gal (BHG) because a woman with Big Hair is forever a gal. Bless their hearts, they are true to themselves. Whether they're wearing a statuesque beehive or a frizzy explosion of moussed, permed, fried-and-dyed mall hair, these are women who love Big Hair no matter what the current fashion. And they do suffer for their art. Certain small-minded, "fashion-forward" people look upon BHGs with the scorn and derision usually reserved for serial killers and politicians. BHGs are full of a certain joie de vivre that the rest of us pitiful, chicken-hearted, flat-haired saps lack. BHGs bring glamour and style wherever they go, whether it's a fancy-dress ball or the waiting area of the Jiffy Lube. And here's a news flash for you: Big Hair Gals are not going away. Theirs is a proud, indomitable breed, a breed that will not bend to the fashion whims of others, a breed that keeps hundreds of industries afloat and thousands of people employed.

THE POWER OF BIG HAIR

For some reason, Big Hair will make a lot of men sit up and beg. It's called *The Barbie Reflex*. Here's the proof. Have any power-hungry, tell-all political career-crushing bimbos in the last twenty years had short, sassy, gamine looks? Fawn Hall, Gennifer Flowers, Donna Rice, Monica Lewinsky, and Sherry Rowlands all invested in cases of hairspray and mousse to send themselves and their men to the front page of the *National Enquirer*. Care to be wife number two for that wealthy but romantically misunderstood real estate

the
Big Hair Philosophy

the Power of Big Hair

mogul, dim-but-sweet oil heir, or Wall Street tycoon? Marla Maples, Georgette Mosbacher, Ariana Stassinopoulis-Huffington, and Carolyn Roehm have all proved that the road to love, Cartier, and alimony is paved with Big Hair. Herein lies HAIR MYSTERY NUMBER FOUR: *Who wants to spoil a perfectly good, labor-intensive do by thrashing around in the sheets?* And let's face it—most men would be afraid to put a hand in one of those big dos for fear of losing it.

Sure, people like to assume that BHGs are all evil, husband-stealin', gold-diggin', claw-their-way-to-the-top-with-a-teasing-comb harlots who exaggerate their femininity and their hair just to lure some poor sucker into their devious plan for world domination. But those are just the perks of Big Hair. Another advantage is that, even if a bomb goes off near your head, your hair will survive intact. Margaret Thatcher proved it—she emerged from a bomb blast with her purse over her arm and every hair in place. You may not agree with Maggie's politics, but you have to admit her hair was *there* for her. Zsa Zsa Gabor's career is built on nothing more than Big Hair and a cute accent. She may not ever have been a real movie star and may have trouble staying married, but she's more than many of us will ever be—a cheap wig tycoon with staying power!

Of course, there are plenty of ordinary, decent women out there who simply have that certain lust for life and that need for volume. For these women, there's nothing like the smell of hairspray in the morning. And here's another trade secret that BHGs will let you in on: Proportionally speaking, if you have a pear-shaped body and cottage cheese thighs, your head is likely to look like nothing more than a maraschino cherry on top, reducing you to—well, a walking fruit salad. BHGs are firm believers in the theory that Big Hair distracts attention away from a big butt. Be that as it may, people could still be looking at you and saying, "Hey, look at that Big Hair Gal. She sure has a big butt!" Yes, it takes a certain attitude adjustment to get away with Big Hair . . . unless you live in Texas.

IN TEXAS, BIG HAIR IS THE LAW

Especially if you're, say, stepping out to the D.Q. for a Blizzard. In Texas, they don't need an excuse. Going to the supermarket? Get out your curling wand. Going out to water your lawn? You need a touch-up. Texan women take great pride in their hair. Not just BHGs, they are THQs—Texas Hair Queens. According to an informal survey, there are more hairdressers per capita in Texas than in any other state, despite pretenders to the Big Hair throne—New Jersey, Long Island, New York, and Baltimore. *The Wall Street Journal* has said that 60 percent of women twenty-five and over in Dallas have some form of Big Hair. Also in its findings was the fact that Dallas residents linked loss of hair with loss of power and loss of opportunity in the workplace. That's not all. When that English feller, Vidal Sassoon came to town in the 1970s and tried to foist his trademark short hair styles on them, they up 'n' ran him out of town on a rail. In fact, we've heard that in Texas, if your hair ain't big enough, you too will be asked to leave the state. No, sir, don't you mess with Texas hair. Of course this is the only state in which the comment, "her hair looks like a wig," is considered the supreme compliment. THQs we know have offered theories such as these:

In Texas . . .

∗ You can tell what religion a woman is by her hair. Baptists have big, blond bouf-

---

Texas Church Hair

BAPTIST   **PRESBYTERIAN**   **METHODIST**

---

fants; Presbyterians have layered, mousy, medium-brown hair; and Methodists have very blond pageboys with bangs.

* There is a definite link in the ratio of beauty shops-to-serial killers.

* If you have a bouffant, you have to wear a sequined T-shirt.

THE BHG HALL OF FAME *Gals Who Sit in the Very Firmament of Big Hair*	
Liz Taylor	Barbara Cartland
Jackie Onassis	Barbara Walters
Ivana Trump	Former Texas Governor Ann Richards
	Naomi Judd
	Wynonna Judd

Big Old Hair
Versus
Big New Hair

Reba McEntire

Dolly Parton

Margaret Thatcher

Eva and Zsa Zsa Gabor

Honorary BHGs (see chapter 5)

Elvis Presley

Porter Wagner

Tony Bennett

Wayne Newton

Fabio

WOMEN WHO WILL NEVER BE BHGs NO MATTER WHAT

Hillary Clinton

Ashley Judd

Jane Pauley

Caroline Kennedy

Emmy Lou Harris

WOMEN WITH HEADS TOO BIG FOR THEIR BODIES WHO INSIST ON BIG HAIR

Dolly Parton

Charo

Pia Zadora

Thin Oprah

Tori Spelling

Kathie Lee Gifford

Celine Dion

Big Hair Genres We Love

CHAPTER FIVE

Men and Hair

JUST BLAME JOE

One of the reasons that men need women is because men—the straight ones, anyway—have no judgment when it comes to their hair. A perfect example of this is an industry that women have been shut out of where they should've been welcome advisers. This industry is sports. Bad things happen when heterosexual non-hair-professional males serve as hair role models to other heterosexual non-hair-professional males.

Across the board, men in pro sports have been known to have the worst dos in the world. Take your fresh-out-of-Latvia hockey players with their bad bilevel Billy Rays, your basketball players who shave cryptic symbols into the sides of their hair or insist on novelty colors, your football players with Mohawks, your tennis players with hair like Weird Al Yankovic, your baseball players whose intimidating combination of bad hair and acne scars makes them look like pure country ugly. Don't they know that they have a certain responsibility to their fans? Not "just say no" to drugs. Not just as a role model to children who idolize them, but to the legions of adult males who assume that if their heroes wear stupid hairdos, then it must be okay for them too. Sports figures have made it hard for a man to have a decent hairdo.

It wasn't always so. In the fifties and sixties, if you were a jock or a small boy, there was only one hairdo for you: a crewcut. Long hair, for a jock, was a flattop. The flattop was achieved by growing the hair slightly longer on top of the head, then coaxing the hairs to stand at attention with the aid of a product called Butchwax (undoubtedly called that to allay men's fears of those really nelly waxes). A crewcut was just really short hair that made a boy look like a plucked baby chick, but a flattop? This was a fightin' haircut. You didn't want to mess with any guy who wore one.[1] As a child, I was mesmerized by those perfect plateaus of male hair. I would often lose track of what Mr. Sexton, my sixth-grade teacher, was

----

1. It still holds true today. Look at terrorist Timothy McVeigh. If a woman had been behind that counter at the farming supply warehouse, she would've taken one look and refused to sell him 3,000 pounds of fertilizer.

Just Blame Joe

ROGER MARIS → JOE NAMATH → WILT CHAMBERLAIN → PETE ROSE → DENNIS RODMAN

saying because I imagined his perfectly level flattop being able to support a vase of flowers, a bowl of fruit, an entire still life! It occurred to me only recently that Mr. Sexton's flattop was there to counteract any rumors, since besides being a male elementary school educator, he also taught us (oh, the fortunate ones!) square dancing and cotillion. That was 1968. But in 1969, Joe Namath of the New York Jets came along and changed everything.

The 1969 Super Bowl was not just a contest between the Jets and the Baltimore Colts; it was a hair showdown between "Broadway" Joe, with his boyish charm and his unheard-of-in-sports Beatle haircut, and Johnny Unitas, an ur-fifties flattopped football hero. When the Jets won, it wasn't just another sports victory; it meant that now the sixties had changed everything. It meant that now *even jocks could be groovy!*

The seventies meant Afros blooming in the NBA. Wilt Chamberlin, Earl the Pearl, and Kareem Abdul Jabar bounced balls only slightly smaller than their hair around the courts. But basketball players had it easy. Afros looked ludicrous sprouting out of helmets. Pete Rose, of the Cincinnati Reds, looked like a cross between the Dutch Boy Paints mascot and Bizarro Superman. Feminist-hating tennis player Bobby Riggs, incredibly enough, seemed to have taken Pete Rose as his role model, making him even easier to loathe. In the world of sports, when it came to hair, all bets were off. Promoter Don King proved that. If you couldn't raise your own crop of bad hair, then you had to get yourself a bad toupee. Howard Cosell was the king of them all, with Marv Albert a close second.

Is it any wonder, then, that men have an anxiety about their hair? No one teaches men at an early age how to deal with the occasional hair disaster. When they do go to the barber, they talk about anything *but* their hair. A good haircut for a man is usually just dumb luck. Within the limitations that primarily short hair can offer, there are oh-so-many missteps a man can take with his locks. When men can be coaxed into discussing their hair, it becomes an incredibly emotional, angst-ridden topic. In countless interviews, men express this same sentiment about a long-buried hair memory: "I just remembered this" or "I've never told anyone this before" or "If you tell anyone else about this I'll hunt you down and kill you." The whole issue of hair, for men, is an unexpectedly enormous well of angst.

Ironically, however, today those social taboos of the past that prevented teen boys from hair experimentation are gone. Joe is a boy who, at sixteen, has already colored and styled his hair every conceivable shade and shape. "But," adds Joe, "the important thing is to act like you don't care." Ah, is this not the overarching theme of one's teen years? "Like," he says, "okay, you spend a long time messing around with your hair, but what you really want," he intones, "is to look like you just woke up and it was just, like, perfect." I nod in agreement. This is so deeply true. Doesn't everyone want

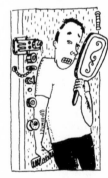 that? "Because," he adds, as though this were self-evident, "you don't want to be like one of those dorky guys at school who goes around with a comb hanging out of his hair all the time." I realize suddenly that I have stumbled upon HAIR RULE NUMBER SIX: *Men need to indulge their hair impulses without anyone finding out.*

A Parting of the Ways

Glenn says he recalls worrying a lot about just the way his hair was parted. As a child, he says, it only wanted to go one way, and

not the other. His mother made a big deal about it. "His hair won't go right!" she exclaimed to his father. Glenn says he worried for a long time that parting his hair on the wrong side meant something had to be terribly, terribly wrong with him. Forty years later, now a

happily married man with two lovely children, Glenn is still trying to figure out what that something is.

The Lollipop Payoff

Jonathan, a friend with a highly developed aesthetic sensibility, complains of his childhood barber. "You'd go in and get the usual butcher job," he relates bitterly, "and then, when it was over," his voice building with anger, "the guy would hand you this lollipop!" The outrage of it all is still fresh in his

mind as he feels he has to explain the obvious to you, "I mean!" his voice cracking, "as though that was supposed to make up for a hideous haircut!"

The Fuzzburr

Greg H. says when he was a boy, on Sunday evenings before bath-time, his dad used to get the electric shears out and give regulation buzz cuts to him and his four brothers while they watched *Disney's Wonderful World of Color*. When his oldest brother lead a rebellion against the short haircut and demanded to wear his

 hair Beatle-style, a compromise was finally reached. Dad agreed to leave their hair long in

the front, with Beatle bangs, and only crew cut the backs of their heads. This was, Greg explains, so that when they got their class pictures taken, there would be the illusion that they had longer hair. They called this style the "fuzzburr."

Fairy Tale

Peter says he could hardly believe it when, in the eighth grade, he finally convinced his military dad to let him grow his hair long. Of course, this meant getting hassled. "Hey," the Roger Maris buzz-cut jocks would taunt, "lookit the fairy!" Cool. Now Peter was a true hippie martyr. The next year, of course, everyone grew their hair out. Through high school, Peter's long hair proved to be more and more unmanageable, but by then he felt pressured by the girls he liked to keep it long. After graduation, he went off to art school and promptly cut it all off. Going back to his hometown for the first time after this, he was instantly greeted by the jeers of the locals. "Hey," they said, "lookit the fairy!"

THE UNISEX REBELLION

With the seventies came disco, big collars, elephant bell bottoms, the shag, and millions of anxiety-fraught men. The solution? The unisex salon, with its supergraphic-clad walls, macramé-clad hanging ferns, and blasts of FM rock, lacked that terrifying pink, feminine taint. Men were hesitant at first, but lured by the Dry Look that only licensed beauticians seemed to be able to deliver, they were soon laying down their heads by the thousands for perms, sets, cuts, and, later, even color. Today, men think nothing of a trip to the salon with their wives and girlfriends. They can thank the unisex pioneers. Here is but one story.

Unisex Showdown

Poor Tom couldn't win. Doubly curse, with kinky, bright orange hair, his childhood was full of "carrottop" taunts. "I wanted to look like Ringo Starr," said Tom sadly. "Instead, I looked like Bozo." But adolescence was even worse—awkward Brylcream moments, and then the "process" that caused his hair to grow in kinkier than ever. Tenth grade, however, started out good. "That  was when everyone began just growing their hair, y'know, just every which way," Tom recalls. He let his freak flag fly. But then the school laid down the law. At least his arch-conservative dad let Tom choose the barber—a hip, swingin' unisex salon. "I want you to cut his hair short," said Tom's dad. "How does *Tom* want it cut?" asked the sensitive-guy hairdresser. They got into a heavy power trip. In the end, the hairdresser made his assistant sweep up all of Tom's beautiful hair and put it in a bag. "You keep this, man," said the hairdresser. "You're gonna want to remember his day." Tom says he cried for four hours. Worse, the next night, he had to go see Three Dog Night with short hair! "Luckily," he says, "it was dark . . . but Three Dog Night," he adds wistfully, "they had these *perfect* shags."

Shag Ball

Mike recalls that around 1973, his high school girlfriend, Connie, while performing a mandatory seventies girlfriend shag-combing ritual on him, found a matted hairball the size of a lemon, deep in his do. "I didn't even know it was there!" He said, adding, "I saved it for a while." And that, dear readers, is the difference between men and women.

Dyeing to Console You

Carl recalls a trip to visit his brother in New Jersey. "I decided to redo my blondness before going into Manhattan," says Carl. He recounts the story of watching Alabama football on TV with an old flowered towel slung around his shoulders while Revlon's "Winter Wheat" percolated on his shower cap-covered hair. "My sister-in-law came in and told us that her grandfather had just died unexpectedly. My memory is of commiserating with her as she cried, and all while my scalp was absolutely on fire from the dye. It stunk too, of course."

Group Therapy

Going to get your ears lowered at the barbershop is different from the intimate *entre nous* of the hair salon. It's a group experience, with an emphasis on storytelling, one-upmanship, and exaggeration. Friends in Oakland, California, tell me of a legendary barbershop there run by—who else?—Tony. Talking separately to two longtime customers, Denis and Hugo, a picture emerges. Says Denis, "Tony was a Portuguese barber with a great mane of gray hair and a pockmarked face who always drove an enormous Cadillac and carried a big wad of cash and a 357 revolver, which he would pull out to show you from time to time—just to let you know it was there." Denis describes Tony's barbershop as "a combination psychological chop shop, barber, and slightly perverse theater. It was like the center of the universe in its own way." Hugo recalls that, at Tony's, there were a lot of hangers-on. "Street weirdos who would sweep up for a few bucks, a genius nerd named Herbie who was about 5´4˝. 245 pounds who would giggle uncontrollably while reading algebra textbooks, and some guys who looked like 1930s Dick Tracy gangsters. And you would always have to wait." Denis concurs with this. "That's when it would get weird. He would introduce these topics, like asking his customers who had been sexually abused as a child. Then he would try to get you to admit that it had been fun, somehow. Or he would demand that everyone tell what their weirdest sexual experience had been, which would force you to lie, of course, so you wouldn't look like a fool." Only if you were a guy, I think to myself. Instead, I just ask, "So, did he give a good haircut?" Hugo says, "Tony treated everyone the same. He'd cut your hair, douse you in Tres Flores, then brush all the hair down into your shirt. If you complained at all about your haircut, he'd just say, "It'll grow back, waddya worried about." I ask Denis if he recalls seeing Hugo, whose not exactly legal occupation, at the time, made him quite popular at Tony's. "Oh, sure. Hugo never had to wait. He always got to go ahead of everyone else. And he always came in with this entourage of women who would all sit and wait, chewing gum, bored, totally unimpressed by the whole thing." I ask Hugo if this was true. Hugo replies, smiling, "Denis tends to exaggerate."

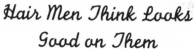

Hair Men Think Looks Good on Them

THE MISSING LINK

THE SHORT 'N' SASSY

JUST CAN'T GET ENOUGH OF HIS SWEET STUFF

MYSTERIES OF THE BARBERSHOP:
What Men Do in There

With the advent of longer hair for men and more elaborate styles, many guys have made the exodus from the barbershop to the unisex salon. Though today they are more and more rare, barbershops were once a keystone in the life experience of every American male. The barbershop was an institution of Main Street America, and citidels of maleness into which no woman would dare step foot, unless it was to deliver her son for grooming. Taking in the Barbicide vessels, the witty showcards over the mirror, the framed picture of ur-woman Marilyn Monroe, she would wonder just how much longer this would take. Finally, to her great relief, her boy is shorn, the tissue collar-protector is plucked from his neck, the barber whisks away the stray hairs, the requisite lollipop is presented with a flourish. She pays the barber, tips him, and scoots the child out as fast as she can. In her wake, the men sigh, rustle their newspapers, and feel the burden of womanhood lifted from their sacred place.

Barbershop Hairstyle Chart

EXECUTIVE CONTOUR • FLATTOP BOOGIE • FLATTOP • CREW • IVY LEAGUE • VANGUARD • BUTCH

JUNIOR CONTOUR • BUTCH • JUNIOR FLATTOP • LITTLE LEAGUE • REGULAR CONTOUR

The Hair Chart

The Hair Chart, which still exists in some barbershops today, proves how much easier men had it in life for a long time. There were, it appears, only seven basic styles to choose from. Fewer choices meant less confusion. No Mohawks, no bilevels, no shags, no foppish Heavy Metal dos. No wonder the world is so screwed up today.

HAIR RULE NUMBER SEVEN: *Never marry a man with hair prettier than yours.*

Hair Men Like on Women

HAIR THAT SLOWS A WOMAN DOWN

HAIR THAT DISTRACTS

HAIR THAT DISTRACTS TOO MUCH

MONSIEUR LE POMPADOUR:
Alive and Well

Monsieur le Pompadour is the male equivalent of the Big Hair Gal. Like the BHG, he cares nothing for current fads and fashions, preferring to follow his own instinct and heart when it comes to hair. Monsieur le Pompadour must have the complete confidence required to ignore the snickering of ignorant fools, fools who wouldn't know a good hairstyle if it sat up and barked at them.

Who is Monsieur le Pompadour? He's the man who exists in a kind of style void, seemingly unaware that there is any other way to wear your hair.

Test: Are You Monsieur le Pompadour?

Do you . . .

* know too much about hair-care products?

* have comb outlines worn in all your pants pockets?

M. LE POMPADOUR

* have a talent for executing surreptitious touch-ups in any reflective surface?

* have hair that stands up to fifty-mile-per-hour winds?

* leave oily stains wherever you rest your head?

* laugh when people call you "greaseball," then get out your knife?

If you answer yes to three or more of these questions, consider yourself Monsieur.

Monkey Men:
ALL-OVER HAIRY GUYS AND HOW TO DEAL WITH IT

BE DARING WITH CORNROWS!

ENCOURAGE HIM TO GROW IT OUT, ADDING A COLLAR AND CUFFS FOR A COOL, BREEZY FASHION LOOK!

TRY A PERM FOR A NATURAL "SWEATER" LOOK!

HAIR GRIEF AND HOW TO DEAL WITH IT: *Learning to Lie Effectively*

Your man is losing it. More every day. He's constantly checking his hairline. You wish he'd get over it. But just think—if it were you, how would you feel? You'd be horrified and obsessed. You'd be searching for hats. Just like he is. What reassuring words would you want to hear from your man? Here are a few dos and don'ts to guide you. And don't forget to practice them, with a straight face.

Do Say

* I can finally tell you. I am repulsed by men with lots of thick, lustrous hair.

* Not all men can carry off that sexy bald thing the way you do, darling.

* Bald men are more virile and more sexually self-assured than men with hair. All women know this.

Don't Say

* Hey, you look like your dad now.

Creative Combovers That Fool No One!

THE "CREATIVE CORKSCREW"

THE "LIVING TOUPEE"

THE "HAIRLESS MOE"

* It's just a more . . . mature look, honey.
* I never noticed how cute your younger
  brother was before.

RUGS TO PLUGS:

The Hair Replacement Dilemma

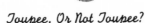

Toupee, Or Not Toupee?

The bottom line here is that it doesn't matter how much or how little money is spent on rug. They're simply not believable as real hair. In the case of, say, Tony Bennett, Tony's fans over the age of fifty-five may enjoy the conceit that their favorite song stylist actually still has a massive mane of Italian hair, so that it reminds them less of their own impending mortality. Burt Reynolds, on the other hand, has been known to play roles without his massive and comic bouffant toupee and is all the more believable for it. For the most part, however, when men try to fool others into believing they still have thick, lustrous heads of hair, they are only fooling themselves.

Operating Instructions: Hair Graft

Hair graft *sounds* like what men suspect women of: trying to bribe them with our alluring and hypnotic tresses. But no, a hair graft is actually just one of the yucky surgical techniques that only the truly desperate (and wealthy) resort to in an attempt to cling to the illusion of youth. The surgeons transplant hairs from the side or back of the head to the top or front. The surgery requires two to four sessions, each lasting roughly three hours and each costing anywhere from $3,500 to $8,500 . . . and that's just till you lose *more* hair.

Scalp Reduction

Here's how it goes: The surgeon cuts out a piece of your bald spot, pulls the edges together, and stitches them closed. Sometimes he has to repeat the procedure several times. (Does this mean that your ears and eyebrows go higher and higher, giving you a look of constant surprise?) Finally, the surgeon covers the remaining bald spot and surgical scar with transplants. A mediocre job may result in the scalp stretching back to its original position, an ugly scar may show until the transplants finally grow in, and the newly positioned patches of hair can grow all which ways. Why am I picturing the post-op patient with bolts in his neck? This delightful divertissement will run you $2,000 to $3,500 per procedure, plus the transplant fee.

Scalp Lifts

If you really want to go for broke, this is the way to do it. They cut most of the scalp loose from your skull and (all together now, "Ewww!") pull it forward toward the front of your head. Later, the doctor inserts transplants to create a frontal hairline. But mismatched sections can be a potential problem, causing your head to resemble a crazy quilt. Besides this, you need more drugs because you don't want to be awake while they're scalping you, and because this is such a big, gross deal, it carries a bigger, grosser risk of postsurgical complications. Your cost? Three thousand to six thousand dollars. Tips additional.

HAIR RULE NUMBER EIGHT: *Sometimes a hat is almost as good as hair.*

Feed Your Head

The first thing to note about the baldness wonder drug Minoxodil is that, in its microscopically typewritten package insert, it states that 40 percent of men using the product saw some new hair growth. That sounds pretty good, until you get to the part where it says that a placebo worked just as well for 35 percent. If you wished for your hair back really, really hard, would that work?

If you're a good candidate for Minoxodil—in other words, one of the lucky people whose hair loss is modest and within the last five years, and for whom it doesn't cause such side effects such as a red or itchy scalp or, um, liver damage, all you have to do is keep using it indefinitely, at a cost of about thirty dollars a month. It doesn't grow hair at your hairline, only on top of your head, which means you become like a living Tressy Doll and take your hair-styling tips from everyone's favorite Stooge, Moe. Another caveat is that any hair the drug does grow will fall out soon after you stop using it. So not only is the crop you've raised strictly *insincere* hair, but if you went away on your vacation without it, you could become your own *Picture of Dorian Gray*!

A fashionable head, these days, is a shaved head, and the only practical option for those men who otherwise would be lost in their own combover nightmare. The other advantage of the bil-liard-ball routine is that it may leave people wondering: Is he inching daily toward death, or is he just one of those really macho young shaved-head guys?

CHAPTER SIX

Did You Mousse Me Much?
Modern Hair Product Technology

RINSE AND REPEAT

Hair-care products are promises in bottles, better living through chemistry, a (comparatively) cheap, quick consumer high. But wake up and smell the sodium laureth sulfate. According to a recent *Consumer Reports* magazine, the original wet blanket of reading material, all shampoos are simply detergents that strip your hair of the dirt and oil buildup that leaves it filthy and lank. It's that unnecessary second shampooing, as dictated by the instructions[1] on every single bottle of shampoo known to man, that you've been doing religiously all these years that can leave your hair too dry and un-

----

1. The instructions for these products, all made and bottled in the United States, are often translated into French, Italian, and Spanish. This is to fool you into thinking that, if it's good enough for the hair of the obviously glamour-superior, it's good enough for you.

manageable. So then, you need to put something back on your hair. And that something
would be . . . conditioner! Conditioners
have ingredients both natural and chemical
that can coat or bond with damaged or processed
hair to make it more attractive and more manageable, but it's only temporary. So, whatever crap you
put on your hair ain't going nowhere. It's just going
to sit on top of your own personal pile of dead protein. "But . . .
but . . . but . . ." You may well sputter. But nothing, missy. It's because we *want* to believe that hair-care product manufacturers
are always coming up with new and better language and more
exotic smells to lure us.

Hair-care product ingredients definitely follow fashion, just
like everything else. Right now the rage is for "natural" additives.
But, says the prissy, know-it-all *Consumer Reports,* there's no evi-
dence that these natural plant agents are any kinder to hair than
those tongue-stumbling multisyllabic chemical compounds. In
fact, these witchy, herbal oils and extracts are usually present in
such minute amount that they provide little more than fragrance.
But such a delicious salad of ingredients! Aloe, kelp, flaxseed. Extracts of chamomile, awapuhi, and rosemary. Extracts of quassia

chips, orange peel, calendula, clove, turmeric. If these don't work on your hair, they might still marinate meat. But if you manage to get out of the beauty supply store-slash-salon with just shampoo and conditioner, you are lucky indeed. Don't forget your volumizer, your humectant, your anti-humectant, your sprizz, your mousse, your foam, your gel, your styling glaze, your maximizing spray. And, of course, there are revitalizing protein packs, rejuvenating treatments, texturizing elixirs. Molding muds, defining cremes, shaping mists. Tea shampoo promises that "tea is an astringent that will restore inborn glisten and sparkle." Aussie Mega Shampoo seems to imply something vague involving kangaroos. Another promises its ingredient of carbohydrate-rich pectin will add "strength and structure" to hair. What about keratin amino acids? Sounds like you might hatch some DNA on top of your head.

But let's examine some of those ingredients. We'll start with a little something in shampoo called hydrolyzed animal protein. Now, is that like putting meat on your hair? And what about a product the manufacturer claims "conditions and protects with human hair keratin protein"? Does this mean it was made out of people? Who or what was conditioning and protecting the guy who lost his hair to make this stuff? Are these manufacturers buying the hair they sweep up in barbershops and beauty parlors? I could be in that bottle. And what about placenta? Maybe this doesn't worry you. Maybe you're more concerned about your products being tested on animals. But look at it this way—there's not a lab rat on this planet that couldn't use a more manageable coat, glossier highlights, and silkier, softer fur.

IT CAME FROM THE PAST

Hair product advertising: In the 1950s, "The Breck Girl" was the idealized portrait of a woman and her perfect, shimmering hair. With her porcelain skin and classy good looks, the Breck Girl was a totally unrealizable role model for an entire generation of girls and women. Then there was the TV commercial for Prell shampoo. The fact that a pearl, dropped into the bottle of Prell took a long time to sink to the bottom of the bottle was supposed to be proof positive that this stuff was going to be good for your hair. It wasn't until the golden age of goofy shampoos and conditioners—the seventies—that Madison Avenue wised up and started marketing hair-care products to the chuckleheaded baby boomers. There was *Gee, Your Hair Smells Terrific; Body on Tap* (made with beer!); and *Earthborn*, which came with those stupid Ph strips because your hair's acidity level was something you were

supposed to be constantly monitoring. *Long and Silky* was supposedly formulated for those satin curtains of hair we were supposed to have. Natch, its companion product, *Short and Sassy*,
featured none other than hairdo-queen/ice-skater Dorothy
Hamill in its ads. Then came *Dark and Lovely*, which sounded like a
Barry White song, but was actually a shampoo for black hair.
Aerosol "dry" shampoos made their appearance for those gals
who just didn't have time for wet hair in the still pre-blow-dryer
era. You were supposed to spray this talcum-powder stuff in and
brush it out, rendering your hair, somehow, "cleaner." One had the
unfortunate name of *MiniPoo*. A more popular brand was called
Pssssst!

For a while, everything contained balsam. There were "edible"
shampoo flavors, too-green apple, strawberry, and one called
Lemon Up, with a citrus-shaped cap, that promised the juice of
one whole lemon in every bottle. But, above all, in the shampoo
heavens, *Clairol's Herbal Essence* ruled. A deep, translucent emer-
ald green, it came in a bottle with underground-cartoony flowers
on it. Its fragrance was the scent of the seventies, a chemically
manufactured wooded glade as smelled through a haze of strawberry Bubblicious on the palate of a thirteen-year-old girl. And
speaking of bubblegum, the required shampoo for all genuine

hippies was a Bazooka-scented product called, of course, *Head*.

One of the more earth-shattering concerns of the seventies were split ends. Apparently, since a large segment of the population had considered cutting or styling their hair politically incorrect after 1968, we were a nation of ratty hair.

BLOW ME AWAY, DUDE

Of course, anyone who actually lived through the 1970s is aware that the major cultural contribution to the era was the blow-dryer. Although this invention had come along decades earlier, in unwieldy metal models, most people had been using those shower-cap-attached-to-the-hot-air-hose jobs, the home version of beauty parlor dryer hoods. Many a teenage head covered with curlers was dried this way, probably during a slumber party while perched on a French provincial canopy bed in a baby-doll nightie while talking to a really cute boy on a Princess phone. It was either sit for at least an hour with a hot-air bag over your head, the elastic digging into your forehead, or walk around in curlers all day, like some women actually did, looking like a big-headed, chain-smoking alien wearing a chiffon scarf. The only other solution was to sleep in your curlers, as though rest was a possibility with plastic rollers or nylon bristles imbedding themselves in your scalp.

Lightweight, cheap plastic blow-dryers, with the power of 1500 watts, caused an absolute hair revolution, changing hairstyling forever and ushering in the dry look. Now instead of having their hair set, permed, lacquered, pomaded, processed, and sprayed within an inch of their lives, men and women alike could have their clean, healthy, shiny hair magically molded into crests and feathered waves. Hot rollers came along to speed up the beauty process in the seventies, likewise curling irons. Curling irons had been around in one form or another since—well, remember *Little Women?* But now they were electrified and jacketed in hot-pink plastic. Styling combs preceded "finger" attachments on blow-dryers, and then there were also hot combs. Perhaps one of the more insidious inventions of the eighties, and a staple of every Valley Girl's purse, was the crimping iron, guaranteed to give a big, annoyingly frizzy do to anyone with limp, flat hair.

SCARY HAIR THINGS
OF YESTERYEAR

Swimmingly

Other than occasionally seen protecting the hairdos of elderly women in condo complex pools in Florida, swim caps are a rare sight these days. Thanks to better-designed pool filters, and the blow-dryer, women aren't as concerned as they used to be about getting their hair wet. Sure, there are still the Speedo variety, but those are for serious swimmers concerned more with swiftness than the fact that they look like condoms. The fantastically decorated latex rubber variety, wittily encrusted with multicolored rubber flowers, fringey fright-wiglike extensions, or odd French ticklerish nubbins, were considered high fashion in the fifties and into the sixties, a more formal time when ladies still wore headgear. After all, since women wore hats every other place, why not in

the water too? Shapely glamour gals in movies were often pictured by the pool, jauntily tucking their tresses into one. After the blow-dryer had taken hold, elderly women with elaborate dos were the only ones left to wear these delightful confections, which didn't help their image. Yes, the decorative bathing cap has gone the way of the button hook, the typewriter, and the dial phone.

Rats and Snoods

No, this is not the name of a cartoon on Nickelodeon. Rats were, originally, balls of hair that women around the turn of the century would save up from their hairbrushes in a fancy little jar, a "hair receiver," on their dresser that, once enough was accumulated, they would use as ballast under their big Gibson Girl dos, a sort of "hair helper." They evolved, more hygienically, into strange nylon donuts through which women would stick their hair and wrap it around to form buns. They can still be found in dusty wrappers on the back shelves of Woolworth's.

Snoods, also popular in the Victorian era, and then again in the 1940s, were essentially little crocheted nets for women to jam their hair into instead of just having a bun or a ponytail. The snood would form, on the back of the head or the nape of the neck, a bag-o-hair. So attractive! When designers run out of ideas, snoods, like capes and knickers, are a kind of goofy distraction they offer us until inspiration strikes once more.

Did You Want Fries with That?

Hairnets are another almost completely outdated hair product of yesteryear. You used to be able to buy them for a dime or a quarter at the corner drugstore, where they'd been sitting for twenty-five years, just waiting for someone who had just landed an entry-level, grindingly dull, laborious, minimum-wage food-service job. The creepy, spider-webbish thing may have blened in, almost undetectable, in your hair, but the dark elastic band against your pale scalp was the dead giveaway that screamed "Cafeteria Lady!" Today, you can still occasionally see buzz-cut teenage fast-food employees wearing hairnets and an expression that says, "Don't ask."

I'm Just Talkin' Bout Shaft!

Often mistaken by upper-crust White Anglo-Saxon Protestants as the angel food cake cutter missing from their silver service, the Afro pick was the one thing in the 1970s a fine brown bro' or a foxy

sistah couldn't leave the house without. It was essential for forcing
their "natural" into a perfect
globe of hair and, in more than
one blaxploitation movie, was also
employed as a weapon.

HAIR SUCKERS

Tap Teaser, Flowbee, Braidini, Rio: Are they bottom-of-the-barrel
Hanna-Barbera cartoon characters from the late seventies? No,
these are all hair products advertised on cable TV, in the wee small
hours, when anything seems like a good idea. The revolutionary
new Tap Teaser is apparently just a cheap forty-nine-cent ratting
comb revisited. "Taptaptap—sides get body, taptaptap—bangs
get bigger!" What's worse than making a complete snarl of your
hair and then covering it up with more hair? How about cutting
your hair unevenly with a dull razor while it's being blown side-
ways? Wow, sounds great! That's Flowbee. Braidini claims to make
French braiding easy, but from the commercial, it still looks like
you need about four more hands to do the job. Topsy Tail was just

a big U-shaped piece of wire that threaded a ponytail through it-self to form a sort of twist. Order Secret Hair and you'd get a whole kit of removable hair extensions that you were supposed to simply and easily tuck into your own hair.

The cozy kaffeeklatsch style of infomercials reared its head in the late 1980s to sell a few million bottles of gunk. They almost always featured hair icon and singer-actress Cher as just one of the many chicks sittin' around talking about hair. Many people with bad hair and low self-esteem found themselves making the 800 number call in the wee small hours.

But consider Rio: not a place, but a hair-straightening product for black hair. Its infomercial featured first skeptical, then thrillingly shocked, customers with an almost revival-tent zeal for Rio. They would rhapsodize, joy-struck, tears rolling down their faces, about the amazing ability of this product to turn their nappy wool into lustrous curtains of ebony. Rio was supposedly made with all-natural rain forest plant products. There was such a demand for Rio that it was back-ordered into the next decade.

This was the product for which black women had been searching all their lives. Apparently, it did work really well for a few weeks or months, until users of Rio started to lose their hair by the bushel. The company that manufactured Rio was swamped with lawsuits and investigations. Worst of all, God-knows-how-many women had to wait for their hair to grow back, knowing, when it did, that it was back to the same old process.

THE SAME OLD PROCESS

Being that the issue of black hair, a type of hair that patently refuses to take orders from the eurocentric world, is an entire and enormous subject in itself, it would be difficult to touch on the subject even briefly, without going into it in depth. Black men and women spend amounts of time in salons and at home that are unheard of to white folks. Whether going for beautiful African, sculptured styles, hundreds of tiny braided extensions, cornrows, weaves, marcel waves, or processes, African Americans must devote many more hours and a great deal more

money weekly to hair upkeep. The result is that salons and barbershops that specialize in black hair become real community
centers where gossip, advice, rumors, jokes, storytelling, perfor-
mance, and sheer hair bonding abound. As time-consuming as it
is to deal with, black folks can console themselves with the fact
that lots of people with lank, wispy locks wish that they had hair
that could be sculpted, like topiary, into any imaginable shape.

EPILOGUE

To Hair Is Human

On the surface, hair seems to be a frivolous subject. Torn between suppressing our vanity and the onslaught of idealized
media images of the perfectly coiffed, is it any wonder we drive
ourselves mad? What are other people thinking? Is it that bad?
Are they working hard at restraining themselves from blurting
out, "What were you thinking?" Is your hair distracting them
from thinking about world peace, a cure for cancer, the meaning
of life, and what a wonderful human being you are underneath
your bad hair? How much can it all possibly matter? I leave you
with one last story that perfectly illustrates our final **HAIR RULE
NUMBER NINE:** *No one is ever happy with their hair.*

Ann tells of the time her hairdresser used too much relaxer on her hair and most of it fell out in enormous clumps, leaving only pathetic, overprocessed patches. Seeking to rectify the situation, her stylist was gamely trying to attach extensions to what little was left and comb it over the bald spots. Just as Ann and her beautician were gazing sadly in the mirror at what was left of her hair, a beautiful young blonde passed by. She stopped dead in her tracks, pointed at Ann, and said, "THAT'S what I want my hair to look like!"

Made in the USA
Middletown, DE
07 October 2020